TELECOURSE GUIDE
FOR

CHOICES & CHANGE

MACROECONOMICS

RANITA WYATT
Dallas County Community College District

DALLAS TeleLearning
Dallas County Community College District
R. Jan LeCroy Center for Educational Telecommunications

Worth Publishers

The Design and Production Team

Assistant Chancellor/LeCroy Center: Pamela K. Quinn
Economics Content Specialist: Ranita Wyatt
Field Producer: Linda Dippel
Project Director: Craig Mayes
Producer: Ken Harrison
Instructional Designer: Janice Christophel
Director of Product Design: Julia Brandt
Producer's Assistant: Manuel Vasquez
Telecommunications Information Specialist: Evelyn J. Wong
Course Development Consultants: Gus Herring, John Pharr
Research Assistant: James Murphy
Media Content Assistant: Brenda Wilson

Telecourse Guide ISBN: 0-7167-5133-X
Copyright © 2001 by Dallas County Community College District.

DALLAS TeleLearning
9596 Walnut Street
Dallas, Texas 75243

Printed in the United States of America
10 9 8 7 6 5 4 3

Worth Publishers
41 Madison Avenue
New York, New York 10010

Contents

To the Student

Dear Student:

You are about to begin a course that will challenge you and encourage you to look at everyday events in an economic perspective. Macroeconomics is a look at the economy as a whole, which requires that we look back in history to see how events and past actions have influenced where we are now. This telecourse guide integrates the textbook and video lessons to help you meet this challenge and successfully complete this course.

The video programs are documentary style, incorporating experts from academia, business, and government entities from across the United States. These experts bring to life the theories presented in the textbook. You, as the owner of scarce resources, as a consumer, or as a businessperson, should recognize many of the behaviors and explanations presented in the lessons.

Economics is an exciting and intriguing social science. My goal in developing this course is to empower you to make intelligent decisions that increase economic well-being by understanding economic relationships.

—Ranita Wyatt

Telecourse Organization

Choices & Change: Macroeconomics is designed as a comprehensive learning package consisting of three elements: telecourse guide, textbook, and video programs.

TELECOURSE GUIDE

The guide for this telecourse is:

Wyatt, Ranita. *Telecourse Guide for Choices & Change: Macroeconomics*. New York: Worth Publishers, 2001.

This telecourse guide acts as your daily instructor. For each lesson it gives you an Overview, Lesson Assignments, Lesson Objectives, Lesson Focus Points, a Practice Test, and an Answer Key. If you follow the telecourse guide recommendations and study each lesson carefully, you should successfully meet all of the requirements for this course.

TEXTBOOK

In addition to the telecourse guide, the textbook required for this course is:

Tregarthen, Timothy, and Libby Rittenberg. *Macroeconomics*, 2nd ed. New York: Worth Publishers, 2000.

VIDEO PROGRAMS

The video program series for this telecourse is:

Choices & Change: Macroeconomics.

Each video program is correlated with the telecourse guide and the reading assignment for that lesson. Be sure to read the Video Focus Points in the telecourse guide before you watch the program. The video programs are presented in a documentary format and are designed to bring analysis and perspective to the issues being discussed. Watch them closely.

If the programs are broadcast more than once in your area, or if video- or audiotapes are available at your college, you might find it helpful to watch the video programs more than once or listen to an audiotape for review. Also, you may tape the programs for review or viewing at a convenient time. Since examination questions will be taken from the video programs as well as from the reading, careful attention to both is vital to your success.

TELECOURSE PLUS

An online interactive option is available to students whose institutions have opted to license it. The web activities are useful for working with "real-time" information related to the lesson content and objectives. If your course includes this PLUS component, please contact your instructor for the course website address and required password.

Telecourse Guidelines

Follow these guidelines as you study the material presented in each lesson:

1. **OVERVIEW:**
   Read the Overview for an introduction to the lesson material.

2. **LESSON ASSIGNMENTS:**
   Review the Lesson Assignments in order to schedule your time appropriately. Pay careful attention, as the titles and numbers of the textbook chapter, the telecourse guide lesson, and the video program may be different from one another.

3. **LESSON OBJECTIVES:**
   To get the most from your reading, review the Lesson Objectives in the telecourse guide; then read the assignment.

4. **LESSON FOCUS POINTS:**
   The Lesson Focus Points are designed to help you get the most benefit from the resources selected for each lesson. To maximize your learning experience:
   a. Scan the focus point questions.
   b. Read the assigned textbook pages.
   c. View the video.
   d. Write answers to the focus point questions. (References in parentheses following each question can be used to locate information in the text and video that relates to each question.)

5. **REVIEW:**
   The following process is intended to help you retain the knowledge you have acquired in this lesson.
   a. Review the terms and concepts highlighted in the textbook.
   b. Review the checklists at the end of each section in the textbook.
   c. Review the Case in Point examples in the textbook.
   d. Review A Look Back in the textbook.
   e. Complete the following Practice Test and check your responses.
   f. Revisit the text and/or video for any questions you answer incorrectly on the Practice Test.

6. **PRACTICE TEST:**
   Complete the Practice Test to help you evaluate your understanding of the lesson.

7. **ANSWER KEY:**
   Use the Answer Key at the end of the lesson to check your answers or to locate material related to each question of the Practice Test.

8. LESSON INTERVIEWEES:
   These individuals are being acknowledged for their valuable contributions to this telecourse. The titles and locations were accurate when the video programs were recorded, but may have changed since the original taping.

Lesson 1

The Study of Choice

OVERVIEW

The field of economics exists because resources are limited, but the potential uses for resources are unlimited. Therefore, individuals and societies must make *choices* in the use of these scarce resources. Resources are used in the production of goods (tangible output) and services (intangible output). Microeconomics deals with decisions or choices that must be made by individuals and businesses. Macroeconomics analyzes choices from the viewpoint of the society as a whole. In a nutshell, economics is a social science that studies how societies and individuals choose to allocate their scarce resources. When choices are made, individuals receive *utility* or satisfaction from consuming goods and services.

One of the most important economic concepts presented in this lesson is that choice involves cost. Opportunity cost represents the value of what is given up when a choice is made. An individual makes thousands of choices every day, as do institutions and government entities. Choices are affected by many variables, and sometimes difficult choices must be made. The video highlights a school district in Los Angeles faced with making some decisions about additional funds. There are a wide variety of needs and potential uses for these funds. The school board president, principals, teachers, businesses, teacher's union, parents, and students all have competing uses for school funds. Opinions vary greatly on what is best for the school as a whole as well as the individual.

The expression "a picture is worth a thousand words" explains why graphs are an essential element for understanding economic theories and concepts. The graphs are developed in the video, step-by-step, in order to simplify complex relationships. You will reap the most benefits throughout the course if extra effort is spent on becoming comfortable with reading and creating graphs.

Normative and positive views are highlighted in the segment featuring the North American Free Trade Agreement (NAFTA) treaty and the different perceptions of its success. Opinions come from all angles and there is seldom complete agreement. There are many "gray areas" in this ongoing discussion.

LESSON ASSIGNMENTS

Text: Tregarthen and Rittenberg: *Macroeconomics*, Chapter 1, "Economics: The Study of Choice," pp. 1–19; Appendix 1, "Graphs in Economics," pp. 20–37.

Video: "The Study of Choice" from the series *Choices & Change: Macroeconomics*.

LESSON OBJECTIVES

1. Define economics, scarcity, opportunity cost, utility, and the term *ceteris paribus*.

2. Discuss the fundamental economic questions all societies must answer.

3. Distinguish between macroeconomics and microeconomics.

4. Distinguish between normative and positive economic statements.

5. Distinguish between causation and correlation.

6. Explain the use of models in the science of economics.

7. Explain the difference between goods and services.

8. Differentiate among hypothesis, theory, and law.

9. Utilize graphical representations of theories and data for analysis.

10. Create a line graph from a table of data.

11. Calculate the slope of a line from a graph.

LESSON FOCUS POINTS

The following questions are designed to help you get the most benefit from the resources selected for this lesson. To maximize your learning experience:

    a. Scan the focus point questions.
    b. Read the assigned text pages.
    c. View the video.
    d. Write answers to the following questions. (References in parentheses can be used to locate information in the text and video that will help you answer the question.)

1. Define the following terms and concepts: economics, scarcity, opportunity cost, and utility. (textbook, pp. 1, 3, 5; video segment 2; telecourse guide Lesson 1 Overview)

2. What is the *ceteris paribus* assumption, and why is it necessary when conducting economic analysis? (textbook, p. 13)

3. List the fundamental economic questions that all societies must answer. (textbook, pp. 4–5)

4. The discipline of economics can be broken down into two areas: macroeconomics and microeconomics. It has been said that in macroeconomics we are studying the forest and in microeconomics we are studying the trees. Do you agree or disagree with this analogy? Briefly explain your answer. (textbook, p. 8; telecourse guide Lesson 1 Overview; video segment 4)

5. Give an example of a normative statement and a positive statement in the video. Explain the difference. (textbook, p. 15; video segment 4)

6. Correlation is a necessary but not a sufficient condition for causation. Do you agree or disagree with this statement? (textbook, pp. 13–15)

7. Models are abstractions or oversimplifications of the real world. Why do economists use models to establish simple basic economic relationships? (textbook, p. 12)

8. What are the characteristics of a good? What are the characteristics of a service? Use examples to illustrate. (textbook, pp. 4–5; telecourse guide Lesson 1 Overview)

9. Define the following: hypothesis, theory, and law. (textbook, pp. 11–12)

10. Create three graphs. One should represent a positive relationship, one a negative relationship, and one no relationship. Explain each relationship. (textbook, Appendix 1, pp. 22–24; video segment 3)

11. Graph the information in the following data set. What are the intercepts? (textbook, Appendix 1, pp. 20–22)

Good Z

Price (P)	Quantity Demanded (Q_d)
$ 1	50
2	40
3	30
4	20
5	10

12. Calculate the slope of the line from the data in question 11. (textbook, Appendix 1, p. 22)

REVIEW

The following process is intended to help you retain the knowledge you have acquired in this lesson.

    a.   Review the terms and concepts highlighted in the textbook.
    b.   Review the checklists at the end of each section in the textbook.
    c.   Review the Case in Point examples in the textbook.
    d.   Review A Look Back in the textbook.
    e.   Complete the following Practice Test and check your responses.
    f.   Revisit the text and/or video for any questions you answer incorrectly on the Practice Test.

PRACTICE TEST

Multiple Choice: Circle the letter that corresponds to the BEST answer for each question.

1.   Economics is different from other social sciences because it is primarily concerned with the study of _____; it is similar to other social sciences because they are all concerned with the study of _____.
    A.   unlimited resources; economic systems
    B.   human interactions; limited resources
    C.   social behavior; scarcity
    D.   scarcity; human interactions
    E.   people; unlimited resources

2.   The existence of alternative uses of a resource implies that it is
    A.   free.
    B.   scarce.
    C.   expensive.
    D.   plentiful.
    E.   unlimited in supply.

3.   The problem of determining what goods and services society should produce exists because
    A.   resources are plentiful.
    B.   resources are scarce.
    C.   most of our resources are privately rather than socially owned.
    D.   most of our resources are socially rather than privately owned.
    E.   other countries can provide us with most of the things that we now produce ourselves.

4. An answer to the question "How are goods produced?" determines
   A. who receives the goods that are produced.
   B. how tastes and preferences are determined.
   C. how resources are combined in the production of goods.
   D. the quantity of society's natural resource endowments.
   E. the types and quantities of goods and services produced.

5. Opportunity cost is
   A. $10 if the first unit is $20.
   B. the dollar payment for a product.
   C. the benefit derived from a product.
   D. the value of the best alternative forgone when the choice is made.
   E. the value of the best alternative received when the choice is made.

6. One question that arises when determining for whom goods and services should be produced is:
   A. "Who pays what share of taxes?"
   B. "Who gets how much of the economic pie?"
   C. "How can we import more goods for domestic consumption?"
   D. "How can we reduce exports so as to leave more goods for domestic consumption?"
   E. "Should taxes be reduced so that people have more income to spend?"

7. The satisfaction people receive from consuming goods and services or engaging in some activities is
   A. marginal.
   B. utility.
   C. maximization.
   D. economics.
   E. economy.

8. Microeconomics is most likely to be concerned with the
   A. economy as a whole.
   B. activity of large segments of the economy.
   C. economic behavior of specific parts or units of the economy.
   D. economywide trends in unemployment, prices, and production.
   E. "forest" of economic behavior, rather than the individual "trees."

9. An example of a normative statement is:
   A. The rate of unemployment is 4 percent.
   B. A high rate of economic growth creates more jobs for the country.
   C. The federal government spends half of its budget on national defense.
   D. Everyone in the country needs to be covered by national health insurance.
   E. Baseball players are paid higher salaries than the president of the United States.

10. The incorrect presumption that because two events tend to occur together, one must cause the other is the
    A. confusion of economists.
    B. blunder of science.
    C. fallacy of false cause.
    D. error of inclusion.
    E. mistake of scarcity.

11. A tangible commodity that people value is
    A. an economy.
    B. a good.
    C. a market.
    D. a service.
    E. a margin.

12. A theory that has won virtually universal acceptance is a
    A. model.
    B. constant.
    C. hypothesis.
    D. law.
    E. variable.

13. A simplified representation of a particular problem is a
    A. model.
    B. constant.
    C. hypothesis.
    D. law.
    E. variable.

14. Macroeconomics is most likely to be concerned with the
    A. amount of unemployment in a specific industry.
    B. economic behavior of a particular household.
    C. economic behavior of specific parts or units of the economy.
    D. "forest" of economic behavior, rather than the individual "trees."
    E. "trees" of economic behavior, rather than the entire "forest."

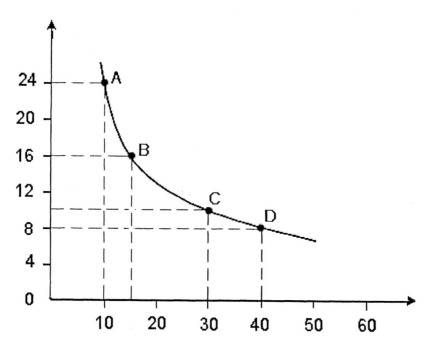

Use the graph above to answer the following three questions.

15. The curve on the graph above illustrates
    A. an inverse relationship between the variables.
    B. no relationship between the variables.
    C. a direct relationship between the variables.
    D. a lateral relationship between the variables.
    E. a horizontal relationship between the variables.

16. The slope of the line between points A and B equals _____.
    A. +8/5
    B. −5/8
    C. +5/8
    D. −8/5
    E. 0

17. The slope of the line between points C and D equals _____.
    A. +1/5
    B. +5/1
    C. −1/5
    D. −5/1
    E. +1

Short-answer essay questions.

18. Create a graph to illustrate the information in the table below.

Income	Consumption
0	200
100	275
200	350
300	425
400	500
500	575
600	650
700	725
800	800
900	875
1000	950

19. What is a possible explanation for the shape of the curve you have drawn?

20. Provide an example of a normative statement from the Los Angeles School District segment in the video.

21. Provide an example of a positive statement from the Los Angeles School District segment.

ANSWER KEY

1. D .... LO 1 .... Tregarthen/Rittenberg, pp. 1–3; video segment 2
2. B .... LO 1 .... Tregarthen/Rittenberg, p. 3; video segment 2
3. B .... LO 1 .... Tregarthen/Rittenberg, pp. 3–5; video segment 2
4. C .... LO 2 .... Tregarthen/Rittenberg, p. 4
5. D .... LO 1 .... Tregarthen/Rittenberg, p. 5
6. B .... LO 2 .... Tregarthen/Rittenberg, p. 5
7. B .... LO 1 .... Wyatt, telecourse guide Lesson 1 Overview
8. C .... LO 3 .... Tregarthen/Rittenberg, p. 8
9. D .... LO 4 .... Tregarthen/Rittenberg, p. 15
10. C .... LO 5 .... Tregarthen/Rittenberg, p. 14
11. B .... LO 7 .... Tregarthen/Rittenberg, pp. 3–4
12. D .... LO 8 .... Tregarthen/Rittenberg, p. 12
13. A .... LO 6 .... Tregarthen/Rittenberg, p. 12
14. D .... LO 3 .... Tregarthen/Rittenberg, p. 8
15. A .... LO 9 .... Tregarthen/Rittenberg, p. 23; video segment 3
16. D .... LO 11 .... Tregarthen/Rittenberg, pp. 22–24
17. C .... LO 11 .... Tregarthen/Rittenberg, pp. 22–24

Short-answer essay questions.

18. LO 10.................... Tregarthen/Rittenberg, pp. 20–21

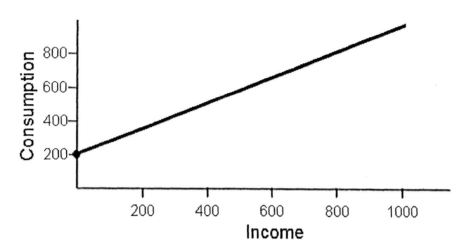

19. LO 9...................... Tregarthen/Rittenberg, p. 22
People tend to increase their spending as their income increases.

20. LO 4...................... video segment 2 and 4
"The most important thing I think we should spend more money on would be after-school programs."

21. LO 4...................... video segment 2 and 4
"The largest share of any school district money is going to be in salaries and benefits."

LESSON INTERVIEWEES

Julia Alvarado, Car Buyer, Dallas, TX
Daniel J. Barnhart, Teacher, Downtown Business Magnet High School, LAUSD, Los Angeles, CA
Bret Caldwell, Spokesman, Communications Coordinator, International Brotherhood of Teamsters, Washington, DC
Victoria M. Castro, Trustee, Board Member, LAUSD, Los Angeles, CA
Steve Condly, Teacher, Downtown Business Magnet High School, LAUSD, Los Angeles, CA
Anita Davis, Student, University of North Texas, Denton, TX
Downtown Business Magnet High School Students, LAUSD, Los Angeles, CA
Soumen Ghosh, Environmental Economist, New Mexico State University, Las Cruces, NM
Gus Herring, Professor of Economics, Brookhaven College, Farmers Branch, TX
Day Higuchi, President, United Teachers of Los Angeles, Los Angeles, CA
Merrill Matthews Jr., Vice-President of Domestic Policy, National Center for Policy Analysis, Dallas, TX

Martin Rojas, Director, International Affairs, American Trucking Association, Alexandria, VA

Mike Roos, President and CEO, LEARN, Los Angeles, CA

Ron Sakoda, Principal, Downtown Business Magnet High School, LAUSD, Los Angeles, CA

Judy Scales, Parent, LAUSD, Los Angeles, CA

Paul Truax, Southwest Regional Representative, Reform Party USA, Addison, TX

Manuel Vasquez, Production Assistant, Dallas, TX

Lesson 2

Confronting Scarcity

OVERVIEW

This lesson develops the production possibilities curve (PPC) which is the first economic model in this course. The production possibilities curve (or frontier) is a graphical representation of the possible combinations of output that could be produced. The curve is developed with the assumption that resources and technology are fixed and fully utilized at a given point in time.

It is important to understand that the curve represents production efficiency in the use of available resources and technology. Resources are divided into three categories: land, labor, and capital. Many economists include a fourth category, entrepreneurship, as an important component. Entrepreneurs combine the other factors of production in exchange for potential profit. If the level or quality of resources changes, then the PPC changes. Technological innovations also lead to economic growth or an increase in production possibilities.

One of the most important characteristics of this model is opportunity cost. If all resources and technology are being utilized efficiently, increasing the production of one good results in a *cost*, which is the amount of other goods that cannot be produced. If opportunity cost remains constant, the shape of the PPC will be linear (a straight line) with a constant slope.

In reality, resources are not equally suitable for all types of production; therefore, opportunity cost increases. If production occurs on the PPC, then the cost of producing additional units of a good or service requires giving up larger and larger amounts of the other goods and services. This effect is referred to as the *law of increasing opportunity cost* and is graphically portrayed with a concave or bowed-out PPC (its slope is not constant).

Although the entire production possibilities curve represents production efficiency, only one point on a curve exhibits allocative efficiency. Allocative efficiency occurs when the combination of goods and services society desires the most is produced. This combination cannot be derived directly from the PPC.

The rain forest segment focuses on the many different uses for the land, the trees, and other resources located within the rain forest. However we may not know the true costs of destroying rain forest from clear cutting and mining. For example, we may be destroying potential discoveries of new drugs or other medicinal miracles.

Production possibilities curves shift outward to illustrate economic growth or inward to illustrate economic decline. These shifts are often caused by changes in the quantity or quality of resources.

The PPC can also be utilized to illustrate the potential benefits from international trade. When countries specialize in the production of goods and services where a comparative advantage exists and then trade with each other, they are able to reach consumption combinations outside their own production possibilities.

LESSON ASSIGNMENTS

Text: Tregarthen and Rittenberg: *Macroeconomics*, Chapter 2, "Confronting Scarcity: Choices in Production," pp. 38–59.

Video: "Confronting Scarcity" from the series *Choices & Change: Macroeconomics*.

LESSON OBJECTIVES

1. Define factors of production.

2. Explain a production possibilities curve and its assumptions.

3. Explain the law of increasing opportunity cost and how it relates to the production possibilities curve.

4. Use the production possibilities curve to illustrate efficient and inefficient levels of production.

5. Distinguish between allocative efficiency and production efficiency.

6. Explain economic growth and the causes of growth.

7. Utilize a production possibilities curve to illustrate economic growth.

8. Define comparative advantage, specialization, and the law of increasing opportunity cost.

9. Explain how international trade affects the production of trading partners.

10. Discuss the strengths and weaknesses of market capitalism and command socialism.

11. Describe the generally accepted roles for government in a market economy.

LESSON FOCUS POINTS

The following questions are designed to help you get the most benefit from the resources selected for this lesson. To maximize your learning experience:

   a.   Scan the focus point questions.
   b.   Read the assigned text pages.
   c.   View the video.
   d.   Write answers to the following questions. (References in parentheses can be used to locate information in the text and video that will help you answer the question.)

1. What are the types of economic resources (factors of production)? (textbook, p. 39)

Production Possibilities Curve

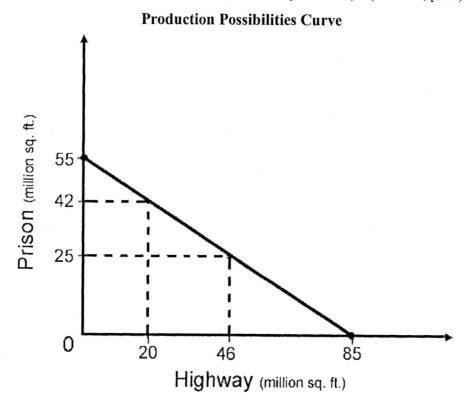

Use the graph above to answer the following three questions.

2. If the state is currently choosing to build 46 million square feet of highway and 25 million square feet of prisons, what is the opportunity cost of increasing prison footage to 42 million square feet? (textbook, pp. 44–46; video segment 2)

3. Using the graph above, illustrate the effect of a technological advancement that requires less concrete to maintain the same amount of strength. (textbook, p. 51; video segment 2)

4. In terms of the graph above, illustrate and explain where efficient and inefficient production occurs. (textbook, pp. 46–48)

5. Graphically illustrate the production possibilities curve for the rain forest example shown in the video. What assumptions did you make when developing the curve? Explain why it should have a concave shape. (textbook, pp. 45–46; video segment 3)

6. Using the rain forest example, explain the difference between production efficiency and allocative efficiency. (textbook, p. 47; telecourse guide Lesson 2 Overview)

7. Use the rain forest PPC to illustrate economic growth. What are the possible factors to cause this effect? (textbook, p. 52; video segment 3)

8. Illustrate a decline in a country's production possibilities and provide potential causes for the decline. (textbook, pp. 46–47; video segment 3)

9. Create production possibilities curves for the United States and Germany in terms of cameras and computers from information in the video. (textbook, pp. 49–51; video segment 4)

10. Use the PPCs created for question 9 to illustrate and explain the basis for international trade. (textbook, pp. 49–51; video segment 4)

11. The two extremes of economic systems—capitalism and socialism—differ in regard to who owns property resources and how resources are to be allocated. Briefly explain this difference. What are the advantages and disadvantages of capitalism and socialism? (textbook, pp. 53–55)

12. What are the major economic roles of government in a market economy? Why is it necessary for government to play these roles in a market economy? Briefly explain. (textbook, p. 55)

REVIEW

The following process is intended to help you retain the knowledge you have acquired in this lesson.

a. Review the terms and concepts highlighted in the textbook.
b. Review the checklists at the end of each section in the textbook.
c. Review the Case in Point examples in the textbook.
d. Review A Look Back in the textbook.
e. Complete the following Practice Test and check your responses.
f. Revisit the text and/or video for any questions you answer incorrectly on the Practice Test.

PRACTICE TEST

Multiple Choice: Circle the letter that corresponds to the BEST answer for each question.

1. The three broad types of resources used to produce goods and services are also known as
   A. economic systems.
   B. factors of production.
   C. production possibilities.
   D. economic efficiency.
   E. financial capital.

2. Capital is best considered as
   A. the natural environment.
   B. produced resources.
   C. financial assets.
   D. human effort.
   E. money.

Production Possibilities Schedule

Production Alternatives

	V	W	X	Y	Z
Capital goods	0	1	2	3	4
Consumer goods	20	18	14	8	0

Use the table above to answer the following two questions.

3. If the economy is producing alternative W, the real cost of producing at X is _____ units of consumer goods.
   A. 0
   B. 2
   C. 4
   D. 14
   E. 18

4. A move from alternative X to alternative Y would
   A. be impossible.
   B. result in greater unemployment.
   C. decrease potential growth.
   D. increase potential growth.
   E. result in greater underemployment.

5. If an economy has to sacrifice increasing amounts of good X for each unit of good Y produced, then its production possibilities curve is
   A. a straight line.
   B. a vertical line.
   C. a horizontal line.
   D. bowed out from the origin.
   E. bowed in toward the origin.

6. If an economy is producing a combination of goods that places it on the production possibilities curve, then it has
   A. inflation.
   B. economic growth.
   C. full employment.
   D. inefficiency.
   E. idle factors.

7. By specializing in the production of a few goods, a nation is
   A. less likely to make efficient use of available resources.
   B. more likely to engage in international trade.
   C. able to become self-sufficient.
   D. able to ignore the opportunity cost of production.
   E. unable to develop a comparative advantage.

8. The United States imports some goods and exports other goods primarily because of
   A. free goods.
   B. unemployment.
   C. self-sufficiency.
   D. comparative advantage.
   E. the law of decreasing opportunity cost.

9. Increases in resources or improvements in technology will tend to cause a society's production possibilities curve to
   A. shift inward to the left.
   B. shift outward to the right.
   C. remain unchanged.
   D. become horizontal.
   E. become vertical.

10. The economy's factors of production are not equally suitable for producing different types of goods. This principle generates
    A. economic growth.
    B. technical efficiency.
    C. resource underutilization.
    D. the law of increasing cost.
    E. full employment of the economy's resources.

Production Possibilities Curves

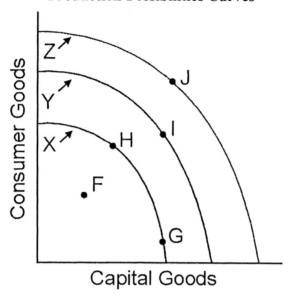

Use the graph above to answer the following three questions.

11. Production efficiency is achieved at point _____ with respect to curve _____.
    A. G; Y
    B. I; Y
    C. J; Y
    D. H; Y
    E. F; X

12. Which point illustrates allocative efficiency?
    A. G
    B. H
    C. I
    D. J
    E. Not enough information

13. Which point(s) illustrates inefficiency with respect to curve Y?
    A. J
    B. G
    C. H
    D. I
    E. Points G and H

Production Possibilities Curve

Use the graph above to answer the following two questions.

14. The economy will experience the MOST long-run growth by operating at point _____.
    A. P
    B. Q
    C. R
    D. S
    E. T

15. The point representing a combination of consumer goods and capital goods that can be attained only by economic growth is point _____.
    A. Q
    B. U
    C. R
    D. V
    E. T

16. In a market capitalist economy,
    A. there is no government intervention.
    B. resources are government owned, but individuals make some decisions over their use.
    C. resources are government owned, and government exercises broad power over their use.
    D. resources are privately owned, and individuals make decisions over their use.
    E. resources are privately owned, but government exercises broad power over their use.

17. Government's role of protecting property rights is considered
    A. enforcing a legal system.
    B. providing certain goods and services.
    C. redistributing income.
    D. maintaining the money supply.
    E. expanding economic growth.

Short-answer essay questions.

18. What does a production possibilities curve illustrate? List the PPC's assumptions.

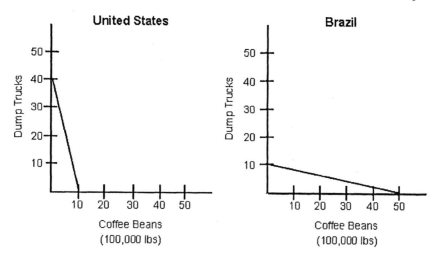

19. Use the PPCs above to draw a graph to illustrate the production possibilities curve if trade existed between the United States and Brazil.

ANSWER KEY

1. B ....LO 1.......... Tregarthen/Rittenberg, p. 39; video segment 1
2. B ....LO 1.......... Tregarthen/Rittenberg, p. 39
3. C ....LO 4.......... Tregarthen/Rittenberg, pp. 42–43; video segment 2
4. D ....LO 7.......... Tregarthen/Rittenberg, p. 39, pp. 51–53; video segment 3
5. D ....LO 3.......... Tregarthen/Rittenberg, p. 45; video segment 3
6. C ....LO 4.......... Tregarthen/Rittenberg, p. 47; video segment 3
7. B ....LO 8.......... Tregarthen/Rittenberg, pp. 49–50; video segment 4
8. D ....LO 8.......... Tregarthen/Rittenberg, pp. 49–51; video segment 4
9. B ....LO 6.......... Tregarthen/Rittenberg, pp. 51–52; video segment 5
10. D ....LO 3.......... Tregarthen/Rittenberg, p. 45; video segment 2
11. B ....LO 5.......... Tregarthen/Rittenberg, p. 47
12. E ....LO 6.......... Wyatt, p. 47; telecourse guide Lesson 2 overview
13. E ....LO 5.......... Tregarthen/Rittenberg, p. 47
14. E ....LO 7.......... Tregarthen/Rittenberg, pp. 51–53; video segment 3

15. D ....LO 8.......... Tregarthen/Rittenberg, p. 51
16. D ....LO 10........ Tregarthen/Rittenberg, p. 54
17. A ....LO 11........ Tregarthen/Rittenberg, p. 55

Short-answer essay questions.

18. LO 2....................... Tregarthen/Rittenberg, pp. 42–43; video segment 2
    A production possibilities curve is developed with the assumptions that
    a. resources are fixed
    b. technology is fixed
    c. resources and technology are used efficiently
    d. only two types of goods are being produced

    The PPC illustrates different combinations of the maximum output that can be produced
    given the level of resources and technology and assuming efficient use of those inputs.

19. LO 9....................... Tregarthen/Rittenberg, pp. 49–51; video segments 4 and 5

LESSON INTERVIEWEES

Sterling Gordon, Director of Quality Assurance, Coffee Holding Company, Inc., Brooklyn, NY

William C. Gruben, Chief International Economist, Federal Reserve Bank of Dallas, Dallas, TX

Jack Lascar, Vice-President of Investor Relations, Terex Corporation, Westport, CT

Linwood Pendleton, Assistant Professor of Economics, University of Southern California, Los Angeles, CA

Russell Pollero, Owner, Friendly Forest Products, Miami, FL

Libby Rittenberg, Professor of Economics, Colorado College, Colorado Springs, CO

Lesson 3

Supply and Demand

OVERVIEW

This lesson presents one of the most important tools for economic analysis: supply and demand. The textbook presents all the mechanics of the supply and demand curves; however, to assist you in understanding the graphs, the video develops the curves and illustrates how to use the curves for analysis. Equilibrium price and quantity are important concepts for you to understand. Determining the changes in equilibrium due to changes in supply and/or demand is also essential.

The video starts with the step-by-step development of the curves through the graphing of a generic demand curve. Knowing the difference between a *change in demand* (the curve shifts due to a change in a determinant) and a *change in quantity demanded* (a movement along the curve due to a change in price) is essential. After the demand curve development segment, we move into a segment illustrating a consumer's demand for landscaping plants for a small suburban neighborhood backyard. Watch for factors that cause a change in demand for particular kinds of plants.

Next is the step-by-step development of a supply curve. As in the demand curve, knowing the difference between a *change in supply* (the curve shifts due to a change in a determinant) and a *change in quantity supplied* (a movement along the curve due to a change in price) is essential. After the supply curve development, we move back to the landscaping example but from the producer's point of view (supply). Watch for factors that cause a change in supply. Then, the supply and demand curves are utilized to find equilibrium price and quantity. This segment also illustrates shifting the curves and determining the changes in equilibrium as a result of the shifts.

The interviews in the State Fair segment focus on how owners determine prices and quantities offered for sale. Notice that although some of the vendors cannot immediately respond to shortages or surpluses of the good or service they are offering, the Belgian waffle maker can. The livestock segment focuses on the reason people show their animals. Winning translates into an increase in the value of the animal and, therefore, the price received for the livestock in the auction increases.

The last part of this video provides examples of markets that do not achieve equilibrium due to outside forces such as government price controls. Usury laws and limits on interest rates are examples of a price ceiling (legal maximum price) which leads to a shortage of loanable funds. Minimum wage is an example of a price floor (legal minimum price) which many will argue causes surpluses of labor or unemployment. As in most subjects, there is disagreement over the usefulness and desirability of price controls.

Your understanding of and ability to utilize supply and demand curves as tools for economic analysis are essential at this point for success in this course. If you do not have a firm grasp of this material at the end of the lesson, please contact your instructor.

LESSON ASSIGNMENTS

Text: Tregarthen and Rittenberg: *Macroeconomics*, Chapter 3, "Demand and Supply,"
        pp. 60–83, and Chapter 4, "Applications of Demand and Supply," pp. 84–101.

Video: "Supply and Demand" from the series *Choices & Change*: *Macroeconomics*.

LESSON OBJECTIVES

1. Define demand.

2. Explain the difference between a change in demand and a change in quantity demanded.

3. Explain how price affects the demand curve.

4. Create a demand curve from a demand schedule.

5. Explain how the demand shifters (determinants of demand) affect the demand curve.

6. Define supply.

7. Explain the difference between a change in supply and a change in quantity supplied.

8. Explain how price affects the supply curve.

9. Create a supply curve from a supply schedule.

10. Explain how the supply shifters (determinants of supply) affect the supply curve.

11. Use supply and demand curves to find equilibrium price and quantity.

12. Calculate shortages and surpluses that occur when market price does not equal equilibrium price.

13. Explain how shortages and surpluses are eliminated in a market economy.

14. Explain what happens to equilibrium price and quantity when there is a change in supply, demand, or both.

15. Explain the effect of a price floor on a market.

16. Explain the effect of a price ceiling on a market.

LESSON FOCUS POINTS

The following questions are designed to help you get the most benefit from the resources selected for this lesson. To maximize your learning experience:

   a. Scan the focus point questions.
   b. Read the assigned text pages.
   c. View the video.
   d. Write answers to the following questions. (References in parentheses can be used to locate information in the text and video that will help you answer the question.)

1. What is a demand curve? What is the result of a change in price? (textbook, pp. 61–62; video segment 2)

2. List the determinants (demand shifters) of demand and explain how they affect the demand curve. (textbook, pp. 63–64; video segment 2)

3. The following list of prices and corresponding quantities demanded (Q_D) is referred to as a demand schedule. Graph the demand schedule, placing price on the vertical axis and quantity demanded on the horizontal axis. (textbook, p. 61; video segment 2)

Price	Q_D
$10.00	20
11.00	18
12.00	16
13.00	14
14.00	12
15.00	10

4. Illustrate the difference between a change in demand and a change in quantity demanded on the demand curve from the previous question. (textbook, pp. 61–63; video segment 2)

5. What is a supply curve? What is the result of a change in price? (textbook, pp. 67–68; video segment 3)

6. List the determinants (supply shifters) of supply and explain how they affect the supply curve. (textbook, pp. 68–70; video segment 3)

7. The following list of prices and corresponding quantities supplied (Q_S) is referred to as a supply schedule. Graph the supply schedule, placing price on the Y-axis (vertical) and quantity supplied on the X-axis (horizontal). (textbook, p. 67; video segment 3)

Price	Q_S
$10.00	10
11.00	13
12.00	16
13.00	19
14.00	21
15.00	24

8. Illustrate the difference between a change in supply and a change in quantity supplied on the supply curve from the previous question. (textbook, pp. 67–69; video segment 3)

9. Include the demand curve you created from question #3 and the supply curve you created from question #7 on the same graph. Equilibrium occurs at the intersection of supply and demand or where quantity supplied and quantity demanded are equal. Highlight this point on your graph. What is the equilibrium price and quantity? (textbook, p. 72; video segment 4)

10. Utilize the supply and demand curves from question #9 to calculate the effect if the market price is $14. Is there a shortage or a surplus? How much? If price is $11, what is the resulting shortage or surplus? (textbook, pp. 72–74; video segment 4)

11. At any price above equilibrium, the result will be a surplus. Explain the process a freely operating market will experience to eliminate a surplus. Include changes in quantities demanded and supplied. (textbook, p. 73; video segment 4)

12. At any price below equilibrium, the result will be a shortage. Explain the process a freely operating market will experience to eliminate a shortage. Include changes in quantities demanded and supplied. (textbook, pp. 73–74; video segment 4)

13. Draw graphs to demonstrate each of the following: (textbook, p. 74; video segment 4)
    A. an increase in demand; illustrate what happens to equilibrium price and quantity.
    B. a decrease in demand; illustrate what happens to equilibrium price and quantity.
    C. an increase in supply; illustrate what happens to equilibrium price and quantity.
    D. a decrease in supply; illustrate what happens to equilibrium price and quantity.

14. Draw an upward sloping supply curve and a downward sloping demand curve. Utilize these curves to determine changes in equilibrium price and quantity from changes in both supply and demand curves. Which examples depend on the magnitude of the shifts in order to determine the change in price or quantity? (textbook, pp. 76–77)

15. Briefly explain the result of government-imposed prices as contrasted with prices determined by supply and demand. (textbook, pp. 89–94; video segment 5)

16. Define a price floor. Would the price floor be set above or below equilibrium to have an affect on the market? What is an example of a price floor and what is its result? (textbook, p. 90; video segment 5)

17. Define a price ceiling. Would the price ceiling be set above or below equilibrium to have an affect on the market? What is an example of a price ceiling and what is its result? (textbook, pp. 93–94)

REVIEW

The following process is intended to help you retain the knowledge you have acquired in this lesson.

    a.   Review the terms and concepts highlighted in the textbook.
    b.   Review the checklists at the end of each section in the textbook.
    c.   Review the Case in Point examples in the textbook.
    d.   Review A Look Back in the textbook.
    e.   Complete the following Practice Test and check your responses.
    f.   Revisit the text and/or video for any questions you answer incorrectly on the Practice Test.

PRACTICE TEST

Multiple Choice: Circle the letter that corresponds to the BEST answer for each question.

1. The relationship between the price of a good, the quantity people are willing and able to purchase, and the independent variables that determine quantity is
   A. supply.
   B. demand.
   C. equilibrium.
   D. disequilibrium.
   E. production possibilities.

2. Consumer preferences, prices of other goods, income, and demographic characteristics are often termed
   A. market technologies.
   B. demand prices.
   C. demand shifters.
   D. supply determinants.
   E. supply quantities.

Movie Tickets

Graph 1

Graph 2

Graph 3

Graph 4

Use the graphs above to answer the following two questions.

3. An increase in the fee charged for movie tickets would result in a change illustrated by
    A.   the move from f to g in Graph 1.
    B.   the move from h to i in Graph 2.
    C.   the move from j to k in Graph 3.
    D.   the move from l to m in Graph 4.
    E.   none of the graphs presented above.

4. An increase in the price of popcorn would result in a change illustrated by
    A.   the move from f to g in Graph 1.
    B.   the move from h to i in Graph 2.
    C.   the move from j to k in Graph 3.
    D.   the move from l to m in Graph 4.
    E.   none of the graphs presented above.

5. Given that meat and potatoes are complementary goods, if the price of meat decreases substantially,
   A. the demand for potatoes increases.
   B. the quantity of potatoes demanded increases.
   C. the demand for potatoes decreases.
   D. the quantity of potatoes demanded decreases.
   E. the demand for potatoes does not change.

6. Economists know that a particular good can be classified as an inferior good if _____ in buyers' income causes _____.
   A. an increase; an increase in demand.
   B. an increase; an increase in quantity demanded.
   C. an increase; a decrease in demand.
   D. an increase; a decrease in quantity demanded.
   E. a decrease; a decrease in demand.

7. If the price of a commodity increases, you expect the
   A. demand to decrease.
   B. quantity demanded to increase.
   C. quantity demanded to decrease.
   D. demand curve to shift to the right.
   E. demand curve to shift to the left.

8. Supply is best defined as the
   A. relationship between the quantity of a good or service sellers are able to offer for sale and the independent variables that determine quantity.
   B. relationship between the quantity of a good or service sellers are willing to offer for sale and the independent variables that determine quantity.
   C. relationship between the quantity of a good or service sellers are willing and able to offer for sale and the independent variables that determine quantity.
   D. quantity of a good or service sellers are willing and able to offer for sale at a specific price.
   E. price that sellers are willing and able to charge for a specific quantity of a good or service.

9. If the price of a commodity increases, you expect the
   A. supply to increase.
   B. quantity supplied to increase.
   C. quantity supplied to decrease.
   D. supply curve to shift to the right.
   E. supply curve to shift to the left.

Movie Tickets

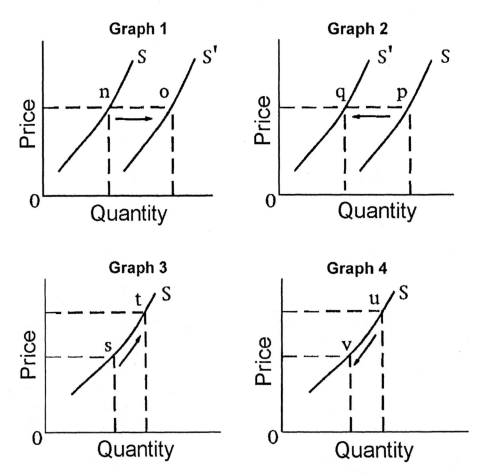

Graph 1

Graph 2

Graph 3

Graph 4

Use the graphs above to answer the following two questions.

10. An increase in the number of movie theaters would result in a change illustrated by
    A. the move from n to o in Graph 1.
    B. the move from p to q in Graph 2.
    C. the move from s to t in Graph 3.
    D. the move from u to v in Graph 4.
    E. none of the graphs presented above.

11. An increase in the ticket price would result in a change illustrated by
    A. the move from n to o in Graph 1.
    B. the move from p to q in Graph 2.
    C. the move from s to t in Graph 3.
    D. the move from u to v in Graph 4.
    E. none of the graphs presented above.

12. An example of a supply shifter is
    A. demographic characteristics.
    B. a burst of new technology.
    C. income.
    D. consumer expectations.
    E. consumer preferences.

13. A decrease in supply is caused by
    A. a decrease in resource prices.
    B. an increase in the number of sellers in the market.
    C. suppliers' expectations of higher prices in the future.
    D. an advancement in the technology for producing the good.
    E. a decrease in the price of a good using the same resources.

14. If the quantity of available housing in a community is greater than the quantity of houses demanded, the existing price
    A. remains unchanged.
    B. rises to clear the market.
    C. either rises or remains unchanged.
    D. is below the market equilibrium price.
    E. is above the market equilibrium price.

15. In a competitive market, if there is a shortage of a product at a given price,
    A. sellers drive the price down.
    B. sellers drive the price up.
    C. buyers drive the price down.
    D. buyers drive the price up.
    E. the price tends to remain constant.

16. In a competitive market, if there is a surplus of a product at a given price,
    A. sellers drive the price down.
    B. sellers drive the price up.
    C. buyers drive the price down.
    D. buyers drive the price up.
    E. the price tends to remain constant.

17. An increase in demand and a decrease in supply leads to _____ in equilibrium quantity and _____ in equilibrium price.
    A. a decrease; a decrease
    B. an indeterminant change; an increase
    C. an indeterminant change; a decrease
    D. an increase; an indeterminant change
    E. a decrease; an indeterminant change

Supply and Demand Schedules for a Good

Price (per unit)	Quantity Demanded (units)	Quantity Supplied (units)
$2.00	350	200
2.50	290	220
3.00	240	240
3.50	200	250
4.00	160	260
4.50	130	270
5.00	100	280

Use the table above to answer the following four questions.

18. The equilibrium price is _____ and the equilibrium quantity is _____.
    A. $2.00; 230 units
    B. $3.00; 240 units
    C. $4.00; 210 units
    D. more than $5.00; less than 100 units
    E. impossible to determine; impossible to determine

19. If the price were fixed by law at $5.00, there would be
    A. a shortage of 180 units.
    B. a surplus of 180 units.
    C. an equilibrium quantity of 100 units.
    D. an equilibrium quantity of 180 units.
    E. an equilibrium quantity of 280 units.

20. If demand increased 50 units, the new equilibrium price and quantity would be _____ and _____ units, respectively.
    A. $2.00; 310
    B. $2.50; 295
    C. $3.00; 290
    D. $3.50; 250
    E. more than $3.50; more than 250

21. If the price were fixed by law at $2.00, there would be
    A. a shortage of 150 units.
    B. a surplus of 150 units.
    C. an equilibrium quantity of 350 units.
    D. an equilibrium quantity of 150 units.
    E. an equilibrium quantity of 200 units.

22. A decrease in demand and a decrease in supply leads to _____ in equilibrium quantity and _____ in equilibrium price.
    A. a decrease; a decrease
    B. an indeterminant change; an increase
    C. an indeterminant change; a decrease
    D. an increase; an indeterminant change
    E. a decrease; an indeterminant change

Short-answer essay questions.

Supply and Demand Schedules for a Good

Price (per unit)	Quantity Demanded (units)	Price (per unit)	Quantity Supplied (units)
$2.00	350	2.00	200
2.50	290	2.50	220
3.00	240	3.00	240
3.50	200	3.50	250
4.00	160	4.00	260
4.50	130	4.50	270
5.00	100	5.00	280

Use the table above to answer the following five questions.

23. Use the information in the table above to graph a demand curve.

24. Use the information in the table above to graph a supply curve.

25. Combine the supply and demand curves from the previous two questions. What is the equilibrium price and quantity?

26. Graphically illustrate the effect of an increase in the price of inputs on equilibrium price and quantity.

27. Graphically illustrate the effect of an increase in demand on equilibrium price and quantity.

ANSWER KEY

1. B ....LO 1 .... Tregarthen/Rittenberg, p. 62; video segment 2
2. C ....LO 5 .... Tregarthen/Rittenberg, p. 63; video segment 2
3. D ....LO 2, 3 ...... Tregarthen/Rittenberg, p. 62; video segment 2
4. A ....LO 2, 5 ...... Tregarthen/Rittenberg, pp. 63–64; video segment 2
5. A ....LO 2, 5 ...... Tregarthen/Rittenberg, pp. 63–64
6. C ....LO 2, 5 ...... Tregarthen/Rittenberg, p. 64
7. C ....LO 3 .... Tregarthen/Rittenberg, pp. 61–62; video segment 2
8. C ....LO 6 .... Tregarthen/Rittenberg, p. 67; video segment 3
9. B ....LO 8 .... Tregarthen/Rittenberg, p. 68; video segment 3
10. A ....LO 7, 10 .... Tregarthen/Rittenberg, p. 68
11. C ....LO 7, 8 ...... Tregarthen/Rittenberg, p. 68; video segment 3
12. B ....LO 10 .... Tregarthen/Rittenberg, pp. 68–70; video segment 3
13. C ....LO 10 .... Tregarthen/Rittenberg, pp. 68–70
14. E ....LO 11, 12 .. Tregarthen/Rittenberg, pp. 72–73; video segment 4
15. D ....LO 13 .... Tregarthen/Rittenberg, pp. 72–73; video segment 4
16. A ....LO 13 .... Tregarthen/Rittenberg, pp. 72–73; video segment 4
17. B ....LO 14 .... Tregarthen/Rittenberg, pp. 74–76
18. B ....LO 11 .... Tregarthen/Rittenberg, p. 72; video segment 4
19. B ....LO 12, 15 .. Tregarthen/Rittenberg, p. 73; video segment 4
20. D ....LO 14 .... Tregarthen/Rittenberg, p. 74
21. A ....LO 12, 16 .. Tregarthen/Rittenberg, p. 73; video segment 4
22. E ....LO 14 .... Tregarthen/Rittenberg, p. 76

Short-answer essay questions.

23. LO 4 .... Tregarthen/Rittenberg, p. 61; video segment 2

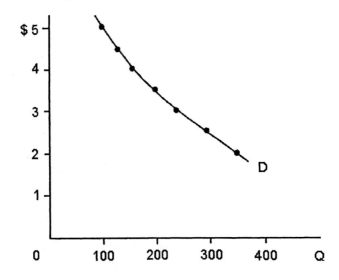

24. LO 9...................... Tregarthen/Rittenberg, p. 67; video segment 3

25. LO 11..................... Tregarthen/Rittenberg, p. 72; video segment 4

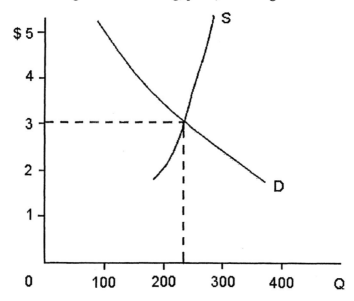

Equilibrium price is $3.00, and equilibrium quantity is 240 units.

26. LO 14..................... Tregarthen/Rittenberg, pp. 68–69 and p. 76; video segment 4

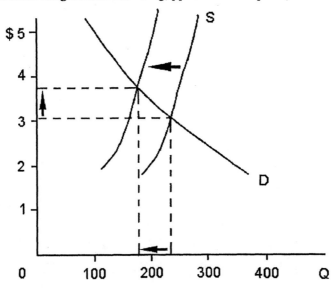

An increase in the price of inputs will cause the supply curve to shift to the left.
Equilibrium price will rise and equilibrium quantity will fall.

27. LO 14..................... Tregarthen/Rittenberg, p. 74; video segment 4

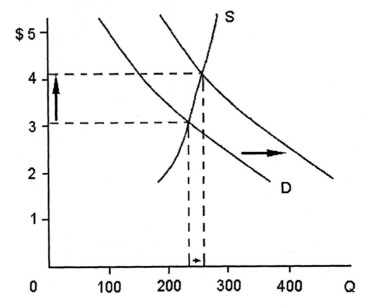

An increase in demand will shift the demand curve to the right. Equilibrium price and
quantity will both increase.

LESSON INTERVIEWEES

Billy Baxter, Owner, Space Roller, State Fair of Texas, Dallas, TX

Jeffery T. Collins, Ph.D., Economist, University of Arkansas, Center on Business and Economics, Fayetteville, AR

Diana Furchtgott-Roth, Resident Fellow, American Enterprise Institute, Washington, DC

Theresa Ghilarducci, Professor of Economics, University of Notre Dame, Notre Dame, IN

Howard Hamilton, Executive Vice-President, McIlroy Bank & Trust Co., Fayetteville, AR

Jack D. Hildinger Jr., Sales Representative, McHutchenson Horticulture and Distributors, Double Oak, TX

Lisa Hildinger, Homemaker, Double Oak, TX

Dennis Poole, Borden County 4H, Gail, TX

Tanner Poole, Borden County 4H, Gail, TX

Norman Zable, President, N.Z. Properties Inc., Dallas, TX

Lesson 4

The Business Cycle

OVERVIEW

This lesson focuses on the phases of the business cycle. The business cycle is characterized by alternating periods of expansion and contraction of economic activity. When the economy contracts, gross domestic product (GDP) and the dollar value of an economy's output declines and unemployment rises. When the economy expands, GDP increases and unemployment decreases. If the expansion approaches or exceeds normal capacity, then inflation is often the consequence. It is important to understand that due to capacity and technological limitations, the economy cannot expand indefinitely. The government often tries to moderate the business cycles in an attempt to avoid the consequences of the extreme fluctuations.

Unemployment is divided into four categories: frictional, seasonal, cyclical, and structural. Unemployment increases during the contraction phase of the business cycle and is called *cyclical unemployment*, which means employment opportunities decrease. When an economy is expanding, more jobs are available and cyclical unemployment declines; however, there still will be some unemployment in the labor force such as frictional and structural unemployment. Frictional unemployment often occurs by choice; for example, quitting a job to find more desirable employment or being a new entrant in the labor market. Frictional unemployment usually lasts for a short period of time. Structural unemployment is due to a mismatch of skills and job locations. This type is usually caused by technological change. Seasonal unemployment occurs when the time of year changes the supply of or demand for labor. For example, the labor force increases in the summertime when students are out of school. Also, there are increases in the demand for labor during the holidays.

If you don't have a job, are you "officially" unemployed? Maybe. Not having a paying job is not the only requirement for being unemployed. In the "real world," there are other requirements that must be met in order to be considered officially unemployed; for example, you must be at least 16 years old, you must not be employed, and *you must be seeking employment*.

The next phases after contraction are recovery and then expansion, which sometimes lead to an inflationary problem. One segment of the video focuses on calculating inflation with price indices and analyzing the causes of inflation. Economists often do not agree on the accuracy of inflation statistics. The lesson includes the controversy over the accuracy of such measures.

"Time Well Spent" is an article from the 1997 annual report of the Federal Reserve Bank of Dallas. The authors of the article look at the changes in the price of goods and services from the perspective of work time. In other words, how many minutes or hours do you have to work in order to buy a particular good or service? Nearly all prices (in terms of work time) have actually decreased over the last century, with few exceptions.

LESSON ASSIGNMENTS

Text: Tregarthen and Rittenberg: *Macroeconomics*, Chapter 5, "The Topics of Macroeconomics," pp. 103–123.

Video: "The Business Cycle" from the series *Choices & Change: Macroeconomics*.

LESSON OBJECTIVES

1. Describe the phases of the business cycle.

2. Explain the concept of a price index and how it functions.

3. Calculate the rate of inflation or deflation.

4. Interpret CPI figures for different years as to changes in cost of living.

5. Explain the limitations of price indices as measures of well-being.

6. Explain why some people gain and some lose purchasing power due to inflation.

7. Identify the types of unemployment.

8. Identify the criteria that determine unemployment and full employment.

9. Calculate the unemployment rate.

10. Describe the limitations of unemployment statistics.

LESSON FOCUS POINTS

The following questions are designed to help you get the most benefit from the resources selected for this lesson. To maximize your learning experience:

   a. Scan the focus point questions.
   b. Read the assigned text pages.
   c. View the video.
   d. Write answers to the following questions. (References in parentheses can be used to locate information in the text and video that will help you answer the question.)

1. Graphically illustrate the phases of the business cycle. Briefly explain some causes of business cycles. (textbook, p. 105; video segment 2)

---

2. What is a price index? What is the index in the base year? If the current year's index equals 138, how much has the price level increased since the base year period? (textbook, pp. 109–111; video segment 4)

3. If the CPI for 1992 is 1.424 and the CPI for 1993 is 1.463, what is the inflation rate for 1993? (textbook, p. 112; video segment 4)

4. What factors influence the accuracy of inflation rates calculated with price indices? (textbook, pp. 113–115; video segment 4)

5. If the rate of inflation is calculated to be 3.6 percent, does that mean that well-being has decreased the same percentage? Briefly explain. (textbook, pp. 114–115; video segment 4)

6. Inflation arbitrarily redistributes wealth and income. Explain how the following could be affected by an unanticipated increase in the inflation rate: savers, debtors, fixed income earners, and creditors. What would happen to a worker's real income if the rate of inflation were greater than the nominal wage increase? (textbook, pp. 108–109; video segments 4 and 5)

7. Define the following: frictional unemployment, structural unemployment, and cyclical unemployment. Which type of unemployment is the most undesirable and why? Could some unemployment be desirable in terms of bringing about a more efficient allocation of labor resources? Briefly explain. (textbook, pp. 117–119)

8. Describe the types of unemployment illustrated by the interviewees in the video, "The Business Cycle." (video segment 3)

9. How do you determine whether a person is part of the labor force? What are the requirements for someone to be considered unemployed? Define the natural rate of unemployment. How is full employment determined? (textbook, pp. 115–116; video segment 3)

10. The unemployment rate is the percentage of the labor force that is unemployed. If the labor force is 100,000 and the number of employed is 96,200, what is the unemployment rate? (textbook, pp. 115–116; video segment 3)

11. The Bureau of Labor Statistics (BLS) conducts a monthly survey of approximately 65,000 households to estimate the size of the labor force and the number of unemployed people. What are some potential problems in the BLS's method of estimating the unemployment rate? (textbook, p. 116; video segment 3)

Excerpted with permission from the Federal Reserve Bank of Dallas 1997 Annual Report, "Time Well Spent."

When a product first comes onto the market, it's typically very expensive, affordable for only society's wealthiest. Soon thereafter, though, its price falls quickly and the product spreads throughout society. Once the good or service becomes commonplace, its price usually continues to fall, but at a slower rate. This tendency shows up in such everyday purchases as housing, food, clothing, gasoline, electricity and long-distance telephone service. It also applies to manufactured goods—automobiles, home appliances and the modern age's myriad electronic marvels. And year after year it takes less of our work time to buy entertainment and services—movies, haircuts, airline tickets, dry cleaning and the like. In a very real sense, the cost of living in America keeps getting cheaper. By harnessing the natural power of income distribution, free markets have routinely brought the great mass of Americans products once beyond even the reach of kings.[3]

EXHIBIT 1: *The High Cost of Living, 1897 Style*

Item	1897 Sears catalog price	1997 work-equivalent price*
1 lb. box of baking soda	$ .06	$ 5.34
100 lb. 16d nails	1.70	151.39
Garden hoe	.28	24.94
26" carpenter's saw	.50	44.53
13" nail hammer	.42	37.40
9" steel scissors	.75	66.79
Aluminum bread pan	.37	32.95
Ironing board	.60	53.43
Telephone	13.50	1,202.23
Men's cowboy boots	3.50	311.69
Pair men's socks	.13	11.58
Pair ladies' hose	.25	22.26
200 yd. spool of cotton thread	.02	1.78
Webster's dictionary	.70	62.34
One dozen pencils	.14	12.47
250 manila envelopes	.35	31.17
1 carat diamond ring	74.00	6,590.00
Upright piano	125.00	11,131.76
Bicycle	24.95	2,221.90
Baby carriage	10.25	912.80

* Prices are in terms of how much a manufacturing employee would earn today working the same number of hours required to afford the product in 1897. For example, a 1-pound box of baking soda sold for 6¢ in 1897. At an average hourly wage of 14.8¢ the typical manufacturing worker would have had to labor 24 minutes to earn enough to buy the box of soda. Today, 24 minutes earns that worker $5.34.

Use the table above to answer the following question.

12. The table on the previous page is a partial reprint of an Annual Report by the Federal Reserve Bank of Dallas (1997). Choose five of the items listed and find their current price in current dollars. Calculate the percentage difference between the current dollar price and the work equivalent price. For example:

If the current price of a 1-pound box of baking soda is $1.29, then the percentage change is equal to

$$\frac{1.29 - 5.34}{5.34} = -.76 = -76\%.$$ The current price is 76% less than the equivalent work price.

Based on your calculations, what conclusions can you draw about price changes over the last hundred years? (video segment 5)

REVIEW

The following process is intended to help you retain the knowledge you have acquired in this lesson.

    a.   Review the terms and concepts highlighted in the textbook.
    b.   Review the checklists at the end of each section in the textbook.
    c.   Review the Case in Point examples in the textbook.
    d.   Review A Look Back in the textbook.
    e.   Complete the following Practice Test and check your responses.
    f.   Revisit the text and/or video for any questions you answer incorrectly on the Practice Test.

PRACTICE TEST

Multiple Choice: Circle the letter that corresponds to the BEST answer for each question.

1. The sequence of business cycle phases is
    A.   peak, trough, expansion, recession.
    B.   peak, expansion, trough, recession.
    C.   peak, recession, trough, expansion.
    D.   peak, expansion, recession, trough.
    E.   trough, peak, recession, expansion.

2. A period of at least two consecutive quarters of falling real GDP is
    A.   a peak.
    B.   a trough.
    C.   a cycle.
    D.   an expansion.
    E.   a recession.

3. The point on a business cycle when real GDP stops rising and begins falling is
    A. a peak.
    B. a trough.
    C. a cycle.
    D. an expansion.
    E. a recession.

4. The expression "too much money chasing too few goods" best describes the condition called
    A. depreciation.
    B. expectations.
    C. deflation.
    D. inflation.
    E. fluctuations.

5. A number whose movement reflects movement in the average level of prices is
    A. unemployment.
    B. inflation.
    C. a price index.
    D. an unemployment rate.
    E. a business cycle.

6. The consumer price index reflects the
    A. changes in the prices of goods and services typically purchased by consumers.
    B. level of prices for intermediate goods and services purchased by business.
    C. level of prices for raw materials.
    D. prices of all goods and services computed from the ratio of nominal GDP to real GDP.
    E. prices of all goods and services computed from the ratio of nominal GDP to current GDP.

7. If the CPI is 120 in Year One and 150 in Year Two, then the rate of inflation from Year One to Year Two is ____ percent.
    A. 10
    B. 20
    C. 25
    D. 50
    E. 150

The Consumer Price Index	
Year	Consumer Price Index
1	80
2 (base)	100
3	105
4	125
5	150

Use the table above to answer the following two questions.

8. The approximate rate of inflation in Year 2 is _____ percent.
   A. 5
   B. 10
   C. 19
   D. 20
   E. 25

9. The approximate value of the dollar in Year 4, relative to the base year, is
   A. $0.67.
   B. $0.80.
   C. $0.95.
   D. $1.00.
   E. $1.25.

10. If the general price level declines while your money income remains constant, then your real income
    A. fluctuates.
    B. increases.
    C. decreases.
    D. remains constant.
    E. will equal your money income.

11. If, in a given period, the rate of inflation turns out to be higher than lenders and borrowers anticipated, then the effect will be
    A. a redistribution of wealth from borrowers to lenders.
    B. a redistribution of wealth from lenders to borrowers.
    C. no change in the distribution of wealth between lenders and borrowers.
    D. a net gain in purchasing power for lenders relative to borrowers.
    E. a net loss in purchasing power for borrowers relative to lenders.

12. An example of frictional unemployment is
    A. an autoworker who is temporarily laid off from an automobile company due to a decline in sales.
    B. a geologist who is permanently laid off from an oil company due to a new technological advance.
    C. a worker at a fast-food restaurant who quits work and attends college.
    D. a real estate agent who leaves a job in Texas and searches for a similar, higher paying job in California.
    E. a corporate executive who decides to retire and permanently leave the labor force.

13. Cyclical unemployment consists of people who are unemployed due to
    A. discrimination.
    B. temporary changes in jobs.
    C. an excess in the quantity of labor supplied over the quantity of labor demanded.
    D. the time it takes for employers and workers to find each other.
    E. a mismatch between the skills of workers and the skills required by the job market.

14. The labor force is all
    A. people.
    B. people under the age of 64.
    C. people working.
    D. people unemployed.
    E. people working plus the unemployed.

15. The natural level of employment occurs if there is no
    A. unemployment.
    B. frictional unemployment.
    C. transitional unemployment.
    D. structural employment.
    E. cyclical unemployment.

Labor Market Data
(in millions)

	Year 1	Year 2	Year 3	Year 4
Population	100	100	100	100
Working age population	80	75	75	90
Number of employed, 16 years of age and over	60	70	50	70
Number not working, 16 years of age and over	10	5	15	10
Number of unemployed, 16 years of age and over who are actively seeking work	6	3	5	4

Use the table above to answer the following three questions.

16. In Year 1, the size of the labor force is _____ million.
    A. 100
    B. 76
    C. 70
    D. 66
    E. 60

17. In Year 3, the official unemployment rate is _____ percent.
    A. 50
    B. 30
    C. 27.3
    D. 10
    E. 9.1

18. In Year 4, the official unemployment rate is _____ percent.
    A. 5.4
    B. 5.7
    C. 13.5
    D. 14.3
    E. 30

Short-answer essay questions.

19. Graphically illustrate and label a business cycle.

20. According to the video "The Business Cycle," why is the CPI an inaccurate measure for changes in the cost of living?

21. What problems exist in terms of accurately measuring unemployment?

ANSWER KEY

1. C ....LO 1.......... Tregarthen/Rittenberg, p. 105; video segment 2
2. E ....LO 1.......... Tregarthen/Rittenberg, p. 105; video segment 2
3. A ....LO 1.......... Tregarthen/Rittenberg, p. 105; video segment 2
4. D ....LO 1.......... Tregarthen/Rittenberg, p. 108; video segment 4
5. C ....LO 2.......... Tregarthen/Rittenberg, p. 109; video segment 4
6. A ....LO 2.......... Tregarthen/Rittenberg, pp. 110–111; video segment 4
7. C ....LO 3.......... Tregarthen/Rittenberg, p. 112; video segment 4
8. E ....LO 3.......... Tregarthen/Rittenberg, pp. 112–113; video segment 4
9. B ....LO 4.......... Tregarthen/Rittenberg, pp. 112–113; video segment 4
10. B ....LO 4.......... Tregarthen/Rittenberg, pp. 112–113; video segment 4
11. B ....LO 6.......... Tregarthen/Rittenberg, pp. 108–109; video segments 4 and 5
12. D ....LO 7.......... Tregarthen/Rittenberg, p. 117
13. C ....LO 7.......... Tregarthen/Rittenberg, pp. 118–119
14. E ....LO 8.......... Tregarthen/Rittenberg, p. 115; video segment 3
15. E ....LO 8.......... Tregarthen/Rittenberg, p. 117
16. D ....LO 8, 9...... Tregarthen/Rittenberg, pp. 115–116; video segment 3
17. E ....LO 8, 9...... Tregarthen/Rittenberg, pp. 115–116; video segment 3
18. A ....LO 8, 9...... Tregarthen/Rittenberg, pp. 115–116; video segment 3

Short-answer essay questions.

19. LO 1...................... Tregarthen/Rittenberg, p. 105; video segment 2

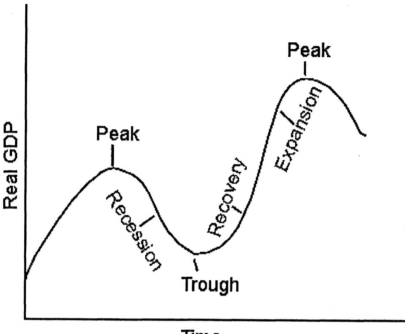

20. LO 4, 5................... Tregarthen/Rittenberg, pp. 110–111; video segment 4
Since the CPI is a fixed market basket of goods and services, it does not account for substitutions, for example, cucumbers instead of tomatoes. The index also does not account for changes in quality.

21. LO 10..................... Tregarthen/Rittenberg, pp. 115–116; video segment 3
Underemployment and discouraged workers are the main problems in accurately measuring unemployment. Overemployment can also distort figures.

LESSON INTERVIEWEES

Frank Ackerman, Research Assistant Professor, Department of Urban and Environmental Policy, Tufts University, Medford, MA

Patty Harvey, Program Coordinator, Texas Workforce Commission, Arlington, TX

Stephen Moore, Director of Fiscal Policy Studies, The Cato Institute, Washington, DC

Barbara Ridley, Manager Client Services, North Texas Human Resource Group, Allen, TX

Libby Rittenberg, Professor of Economics, Colorado College, Colorado Springs, CO

Jennifer Roberts, Planning and Research Manager, North Central Texas Workforce Development Board, Arlington, TX

Wes Taylor, Network Administrator, Q4i.com, Wylie, TX

Meredith M. Walker, Economist, Federal Reserve Bank of Dallas, Dallas, TX

Deborah Warren, Job Seeker, Greenville, TX

Lloyd A. Webb, Executive Director, North Texas Human Resource Group, Denton, TX

Lesson 5

Measuring Economic Growth

OVERVIEW

This lesson begins with the circular flow model, which is a graphical representation of a private, closed economy without government or international sectors. (The international and government sectors will be added in other lessons.) This model will be revisited throughout the course. The circular flow model illustrates the "symbiotic" or mutually beneficial relationship between consumers and producers. (Throughout this course, the terms *businesses, producers,* and *firms* are used interchangeably.) In the simplified version of the model shown in the video, households are the owners of the factors of production (land, labor, capital, and entrepreneurial abilities); therefore, households *supply* these resources to an *input* market. Businesses *demand* these factors of production in order to produce a good or service; then, businesses *supply* the goods and services to the *output* market. In turn, households *demand* the goods and services from the *output* market. These actions represent one of the "flows" in the circular flow model. The other flow is dollars. Households supply resources in exchange for rent, wages, interest, and profit. These dollars are used to pay for the goods and services households demand in the output market. The flow continues as businesses use the sales dollars to pay for the resources used in production.

Segment 2 includes a graphic of the circular flow model. Keep this graphic representation in mind as you watch the video segment about Branson, a small town in Missouri that depends primarily on tourism. This town is used to illustrate the flow of resources and output that make up one of the flows in the model and the dollar flow that makes it all work.

The next segment pertains to measuring economic activity represented by the circular flow model in the economy. The usual measure is gross domestic product (GDP), a term that is familiar to most of us. You will learn about the components used to calculate the value of output or production. You will also learn about some of the difficulties encountered in obtaining accurate measurements. Segment 4 uses the expenditures approach to calculate the value of GDP. The goal is to estimate the dollar value of output (production) in the United States. In this approach, spending on goods and services by consumers, governments, and foreigners (exports) is added to investment spending by businesses. Domestic spending on imports is then subtracted. This sum represents GDP. It is important to note that government spending that is only a transfer of dollars (social security, welfare, unemployment, etc.) is NOT included. Other purely financial transactions, such as stock purchases or monetary gifts, are also not included. Spending on used items is not included since they were counted as part of GDP when the goods were produced. Also note that *investment* refers to *gross* investment instead of *net* investment, which is the difference between gross investment and depreciation.

Segment 5 illustrates some of the problems associated with calculating a true dollar value of production. Illegal activities, barter activities, and the value of do-it-yourself activities are just some of the productive activities that are not reflected in GDP statistics.

Services produced and purchased in the cleanup of pollution problems are counted as part of output. However, their inclusion in GDP tends to distort the measure of how well a society is actually doing.

The last segment illustrates the use of GDP statistics for comparing the standard of living levels in different countries. Per capita GDP is a better measure for comparing the standards in different countries, yet this is not a perfect measure since there are many intangible factors which have value that cannot be measured or quantified.

LESSON ASSIGNMENTS

Text: Tregarthen and Rittenberg: *Macroeconomics*, Chapter 6, "Measuring Total Output and Income," pp. 124–144.

Video: "Measuring Economic Growth" from the series *Choices & Change*: *Macroeconomics*.

LESSON OBJECTIVES

1. Draw a simple circular flow model.

2. Interpret a circular flow diagram by explaining the meaning of each of the flow arrows.

3. Explain why the value of final output equals the value of income generated in its production.

4. Define investment (I).

5. Distinguish between GDP and GNP.

6. Calculate the value of GDP using the expenditure approach.

7. Distinguish between real GDP and nominal GDP, GDP and NDP, and net I (investment) and gross I.

8. Explain why taxes and transfer payments are not included in GDP.

9. Identify and explain the conceptual problems associated with estimating GDP.

10. Evaluate the effectiveness of GDP estimates as a measure of economic well-being of an economy.

11. Evaluate the effectiveness of GDP and related measures as a means of comparing different economies.

LESSON FOCUS POINTS

The following questions are designed to help you get the most benefit from the resources selected for this lesson. To maximize your learning experience:

   a. Scan the focus point questions.
   b. Read the assigned text pages.
   c. View the video.
   d. Write answers to the following questions. (References in parentheses can be used to locate information in the text and video that will help you answer the question.)

1. Use the information from the video "Measuring Economic Growth" to create a simple circular flow model of the Branson economy. (video segment 2)

2. Explain the meaning of each of the flow arrows in the circular flow model constructed in the previous question. (textbook, p. 125; video segment 2)

3. Explain the process that leads to income being equal to output or production in an economy. (textbook, pp. 131–132; video segment 2)

4. In economic terms, what is investment? How do inventories relate to investment? (textbook, p. 126; video segment 4)

5. Define gross domestic product (GDP) and gross national product (GNP). How do these measures of output differ? (textbook, p. 131)

6. Explain the expenditures approach to calculating GDP. (textbook, pp. 125–129; video segment 4)

Economic Data
(in billions of dollars)

Consumption	5,698.6	Gross investment	1,547.4
Government purchases	1,480.3	Exports	815.2
Imports	1,000.3	Depreciation	650.4

7. Use the information in the table above to calculate the following values:
    A. GDP (textbook, pp. 125–129; video segment 4)
    B. NDP (textbook, p. 135)
    C. Net investment (telecourse guide Lesson 5 Overview)

8. What are the implications of positive net investment versus negative net investment in regard to economic growth? (textbook, p. 126)

9. What is the difference between real and nominal GDP? When are real and nominal GDP equal? (textbook, pp. 113 and 136)

10. Why are the following transactions excluded from calculating GDP: financial sales transactions, used goods sales, public and private transfer payments? Why would taxes paid to governments also be excluded from GDP? (textbook, pp. 126–127 and p. 134)

11. GDP may understate the total market value of goods and services produced in a year's time because of nonmarket production and the underground economy. Estimate the value of your productive, nonmarket activities that you do on a weekly basis. (textbook, `pp. 136–139; video segment 5)

12. GDP may not be an accurate measure of economic or social well-being. Leisure time, improved product quality, distribution, and pollution are variables that need to be taken into account when assessing our social or economic well-being. Briefly explain how these variables complicate the assessment of GDP as a measure of social or economic well-being. (textbook, pp. 136–139; video segment 5)

13. Since GDP is a measure of economic performance, it may be useful to compare the real GDP of nations. However, comparing real GDP of nations may not provide insight to a country's standard of living. For example, India has a much larger GDP than Switzerland; however, Switzerland has a much higher standard of living. What would be a better measure of a nation's standard of living than real GDP? Briefly explain. (textbook, pp. 140–142; video segment 6)

REVIEW

The following process is intended to help you retain the knowledge you have acquired in this lesson.

    a. Review the terms and concepts highlighted in the textbook.
    b. Review the checklists at the end of each section in the textbook.
    c. Review the Case in Point examples in the textbook.
    d. Review A Look Back in the textbook.
    e. Complete the following Practice Test and check your responses.
    f. Revisit the text and/or video for any questions you answer incorrectly on the Practice Test.

PRACTICE TEST

Multiple Choice: Circle the letter that corresponds to the BEST answer for each question.

1. The equality between expenditures on final output and income received from final output implies that GDP is
   A. greater than factor income.
   B. equal to factor income.
   C. less than factor income.
   D. equal to personal consumption expenditures.
   E. equal to gross private domestic investment.

2. The value of capital goods and services purchased by a business during a given time period is measured by
   A. consumption.
   B. investment.
   C. government purchases.
   D. transfer payments.
   E. net exports.

3. One reason that investment plays a crucial role in the macroeconomy is that it
   A. is the largest expenditure on GDP.
   B. is the smallest expenditure on GDP.
   C. represents all purchases by the government sector.
   D. represents net purchases by the foreign sector.
   E. is very volatile.

4. According to the circular flow model, gross domestic income is
   A. greater than gross domestic product.
   B. less than gross domestic product.
   C. equal to gross domestic product.
   D. equal to indirect business taxes.
   E. equal to capital consumption allowance.

5. In the simple circular flow model,
   A. households supply resources and supply goods and services.
   B. businesses demand resources and demand goods and services.
   C. households supply resources and demand goods and services.
   D. businesses supply resources and supply goods and services.
   E. both B and C.

Measuring GDP—Expenditure Viewpoint
(in billions of dollars)

Personal consumption	$500
Gross private domestic investment	50
Net exports	–5
State and local government purchases of goods and services	200
Federal government purchases of goods and services	100
Imports	15
Depreciation	45

Use the table above to answer the following three questions.

6. GDP is
   A. $800 billion.
   B. $860 billion.
   C. $845 billion.
   D. $1,000 billion.
   E. $1,010 billion.

7. NDP is
   A. $800 billion.
   B. $860 billion.
   C. $845 billion.
   D. $1,000 billion.
   E. $1,010 billion.

8. Net investment is
   A. 95 billion.
   B. 50 billion.
   C. 45 billion.
   D. 5 billion.
   E. –5 billion.

9. Economic data that reflect actual prices as they existed each year are said to be expressed in terms of
   A. real dollars.
   B. nominal dollars.
   C. fixed dollars.
   D. variable dollars.
   E. historical dollars.

10. A measure of the economy's output in constant dollars is
    A. intermediate GDP.
    B. current GDP.
    C. nominal GDP.
    D. real GDP.
    E. inflation.

11. Payments that do not require the recipients to produce a good or service in exchange are
    A. investments.
    B. transfer payments.
    C. government purchases.
    D. consumption.
    E. net exports.

12. GDP includes _____ expenditures but does not include _____ expenditures.
    A. education; national defense
    B. Social Security; education
    C. Social Security; national defense
    D. national defense; transfer payments
    E. national defense; education

13. One "conceptual problem" of measuring real GDP involves
    A. the service sector.
    B. revisions of data.
    C. household production.
    D. new goods.
    E. quality changes.

14. One "conceptual problem" of measuring real GDP involves
    A. the service sector.
    B. ignoring economic "bads."
    C. revisions of data.
    D. new goods.
    E. quality changes.

Short-answer essay questions.

15. Draw a simple circular flow model. Include arrows to indicate flows and label all parts.

16. What is the difference between GDP and GNP?

17. In terms of the components of GDP, explain why taxes and transfer payments are not part of GDP.

18. Using examples from the video "Measuring Economic Growth," evaluate the usefulness of GDP estimates in relation to economic well-being.

19. In the video "Measuring Economic Growth," what countries are compared in terms of per capita GDP? Evaluate GDP as a measure of economic well-being as it relates to these examples.

ANSWER KEY

1. B ....LO 3 .... Tregarthen/Rittenberg, pp. 131–132; video segment 2
2. B ....LO 4 .... Tregarthen/Rittenberg, p. 126; video segment 4
3. E ....LO 4 .... Tregarthen/Rittenberg, p. 127
4. C ....LO 2 .... Tregarthen/Rittenberg, p. 132
5. C ....LO 1, 2...... Tregarthen/Rittenberg, pp. 125–128; video segment 2;
    .... Wyatt, telecourse guide Lesson 5 Overview
6. C ....LO 6 .... Tregarthen/Rittenberg, pp. 125–128; video segment 4
7. A ....LO 7 .... Tregarthen/Rittenberg, p. 135
8. D ....LO 7 .... Tregarthen/Rittenberg, p. 135
9. B ....LO 7 .... Tregarthen/Rittenberg, p. 136
10. D ....LO 7 .... Tregarthen/Rittenberg, p. 136
11. B ....LO 8 .... Tregarthen/Rittenberg, p. 127
12. D ....LO 6, 8...... Tregarthen/Rittenberg, p. 127;
    .... Wyatt, telecourse guide Lesson 5 Overview
13. C ....LO 9 .... Tregarthen/Rittenberg, pp. 138–139; video segment 5
14. B ....LO 9 .... Tregarthen/Rittenberg, pp. 138–139; video segment 5

Short-answer essay questions.

15. LO 1, 2 .... Tregarthen/Rittenberg, p. 125; video segment 2

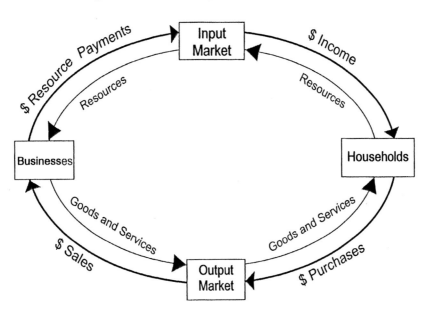

16. LO 5 .... Tregarthen/Rittenberg, p. 131
GDP is the total value of final goods and services produced in the United States in a given time period.
GNP is the total value of final goods and services produced by U.S.-owned resources here and abroad.

17. LO 8 .... Tregarthen/Rittenberg, p. 127
Taxes and transfer payments are dollars changing hands without the recipient exchanging or producing goods or services; therefore, they do not represent production of output.

18. LO 10 .... Tregarthen/Rittenberg, pp. 138–139; video segment 5
One problem in using GDP estimates as a measure of well-being is the value of production that takes place outside of a market. These activities have value but are not counted. Some activities are counted, such as pollution cleanup efforts, but we may not be better off from this increase in GDP.

19. LO 11 .... Tregarthen/Rittenberg, pp. 138–139; video segment 6
The Inuit people of Nunawat are an example of a society with a very low GDP; however, this does not correlate to their quality of life. Sweden is an example with a high rate of GDP, and India, with a very large population, has a low standard of living. Using GDP and per capita GDP estimates as measures of well-being have their problems. They do not illustrate the distribution of output or income. They also do not quantify aesthetic values.

LESSON INTERVIEWEES

Corrine Cox, Dancer, Jim Stafford Theater, Branson, MO

Evan Koenig, Senior Economist and Vice-President, Federal Reserve Bank of Dallas, Dallas, TX

Ester Mirjam-Sent, Economist, University of Notre Dame, Notre Dame, IN

Ann Stafford, Co-Owner, Jim Stafford Theater, Branson, MO

Timothy Tregarthen, Professor of Economics, University of Colorado, Colorado Springs, CO

Lesson 6

Aggregate Supply and Demand

OVERVIEW

This lesson introduces the aggregate supply (AS) and aggregate demand (AD) model, which is a simplified representation of an entire economy. This AS/AD model is useful for predicting the effects on inflation and unemployment from changes in the macroeconomy.

The aggregate demand curve represents the demand for all goods and services by all the sectors of the economy at different price levels. The AD curve is downward sloping because of the following:

- Higher price levels translate into higher interest rates; therefore, spending that depends on interest rates decreases. (Some consumer spending and most business spending, i.e., investment, depend on interest rates.)
- Higher domestic price levels lead to increased imports and decreased exports.
- Higher price levels reduce the value of income; therefore, less output can be purchased.

The short-run aggregate supply curve (SRAS) is upward sloping and represents the amount of output businesses will produce at different price levels. Costs of production tend to be fixed in the short run; therefore, higher price levels are incentives to increase production.

The intersection of the AD (aggregate demand) and SRAS curves identifies the amount of output, or GDP, and the corresponding price level where the economy achieves equilibrium. If the economy is not producing that level of output, market pressures will push the economy toward its point of equilibrium. If the economy is producing a larger quantity of output than equilibrium, inventories will rise due to lack of sales, businesses will cut back on production, and the price level will fall in the model. This will continue until there is no longer a buildup of inventories and the economy achieves equilibrium. If output falls short of equilibrium, inventories will decrease. Businesses then increase production and, again, this continues until there is no pressure to increase production.

Not every equilibrium is a desirable equilibrium. The goal is to achieve *full employment* equilibrium where AD (aggregate demand) and SRAS (short-run aggregate supply) intersect at the full employment level of output. This model illustrates full employment output with a long-run aggregate supply (LRAS) curve, which is a vertical line at full employment or potential GDP.

The third segment illustrates the creation of an inflationary gap due to large increases in government spending on the Vietnam War and President Johnson's War on Poverty. An inflationary gap occurs if equilibrium exceeds full employment output, that is, when the SRAS and AD curves intersect to the right of LRAS.

The next segment continues the use of the AS/AD model with an example of a recessionary gap. Graphically this occurs when equilibrium is less than full employment, that is, when the SRAS and AD curves intersect to the left of LRAS. In this segment, the demand for domestic automobiles decreases and the demand for foreign automobiles increases, causing a decrease in AD, which creates a recessionary gap. These changes in AD combined with an oil embargo caused a major decrease in SRAS and led to an unusual case of unemployment in conjunction with inflation. *Stagflation* is the term representing the simultaneous condition of high unemployment and high inflation. This example also highlights the government's involvement in the private sector to save the Chrysler Corporation.

The last segment focuses on the potential for government to manipulate an economy. The government can use fiscal policy (government spending and taxing) or monetary policy (money and credit controls) to influence the economy. When government officials take action for the purpose of changing economic conditions, it is usually called *stabilization policy*. There are many different opinions as to the role of government involvement in our economy, including economists who disagree on this subject.

LESSON ASSIGNMENTS

Text: Tregarthen and Rittenberg: *Macroeconomics*, Chapter 7, "Aggregate Demand and Aggregate Supply," pp. 145–167.

Video: "Aggregate Supply and Demand" from the series *Choices & Change: Macroeconomics*.

LESSON OBJECTIVES

1. Define aggregate demand, short-run aggregate supply, natural rate of employment, natural level of GDP, sticky wages, equilibrium price level, equilibrium real GDP, recessionary gap, and inflationary gap.

2. Distinguish between movements along an aggregate curve (supply or demand) and shifts in the curve.

3. Explain why aggregate demand has a negative slope.

4. Predict the impact on equilibrium real GDP and price levels of changes in factors that shift aggregate supply.

5. Predict the impact on equilibrium real GDP and price levels of changes in factors that shift aggregate demand.

6. Explain the concept of "sticky" prices and how they affect equilibrium.

7. Describe and graph a recessionary gap.

8. Describe and graph an inflationary gap.

9. Utilize an AS/AD graph to explain the concept of stagflation.

10. Describe and graph how full employment equilibrium may be achieved.

11. Explain the difference between monetary policy and fiscal policy.

12. Explain expansionary policies.

13. Explain contractionary polices.

14. Explain the difference between nonintervention policy and stabilization policy.

LESSON FOCUS POINTS

The following questions are designed to help you get the most benefit from the resources selected for this lesson. To maximize your learning experience:

    a.   Scan the focus point questions.
    b.   Read the assigned text pages.
    c.   View the video.
    d.   Write answers to the following questions. (References in parentheses can be used to locate information in the text and video that will help you answer the question.)

1. Define the following terms and concepts: aggregate demand, short-run aggregate supply, natural rate of employment, natural level of GDP, long-run aggregate supply, sticky wages, equilibrium price level, equilibrium real GDP, recessionary gap, and inflationary gap. (textbook, pp. 145–164; video segments 2, 3, and 4)

2. Will a change in the price level bring about a change in aggregate supply or aggregate demand? Briefly explain. What will cause a movement from one point along a particular aggregate supply or aggregate demand curve to another point? Briefly explain. (textbook, p. 147 and p. 153; video segment 2)

3. Explain the real balance effect, the interest rate effect, and the international trade effect in terms of an aggregate demand curve. (textbook, p. 147)

4. What are the determinants of aggregate supply that cause a shift of the aggregate supply curve? In the video "Aggregate Supply and Demand," what causes the aggregate supply curve to shift? Graphically illustrate the effect on equilibrium price levels and equilibrium output levels. (textbook, p. 153 and p. 175; video segment 2)

5. What are the determinants of aggregate demand that cause a shift of the aggregate demand curve? In the video "Aggregate Supply and Demand," what causes the aggregate demand curve to shift? Graphically illustrate the effect on equilibrium price levels and equilibrium output levels. (textbook, pp. 147–149; video segment 2)

6. What is meant by the term *sticky prices*? When there is an increase in aggregate demand in the economy, the price level can increase; however, when there is a decrease in aggregate demand, the overall price level may not decrease. Briefly explain why the overall price level can go up easier than it can go down. (textbook, pp. 151–155)

7. Draw a graph showing the macroeconomy experiencing a recessionary gap. What is happening in a recessionary gap? (textbook, pp. 158–159; video segment 4)

8. Draw a graph showing the macroeconomy experiencing an inflationary gap. What is happening in an inflationary gap? (textbook, pp. 158–159; video segment 3)

9. What will a decrease in aggregate supply do to the overall price level and output levels in the economy? What term do economists use to explain a situation where high inflation and high unemployment occur simultaneously? Utilize an AS/AD graph to illustrate this effect. In the video "Aggregate Supply and Demand," what causes this period of high inflation and unemployment? (textbook, pp. 159–160; telecourse guide Lesson 6 Overview; video segments 3 and 4)

10. Utilize an AS/AD graph to illustrate and explain how an economy can achieve full employment output, without government interference, if the economy is currently experiencing a recessionary gap. (textbook, p. 158 and p. 160; video segment 2)

11. Monetary and fiscal policies are stabilization tools. How are the two alike and how are they different? (textbook, pp. 161–162; video segment 5)

12. Explain why expansionary policies may be used. Provide an example of an expansionary fiscal and monetary policy. (textbook, pp. 160–162; video segment 5)

13. Explain why contractionary policies may be used. Provide an example of a contractionary fiscal and monetary policy. (textbook, pp. 160–162; video segment 5)

14. Explain nonintervention policy and describe how it differs from stabilization policy. (textbook, p. 160; video segments 5 and 6)

15. The video "Aggregate Supply and Demand" highlights different views from average citizens as well as economists on the subject of government interference in the macroeconomy. In your opinion, what role should the government play in the economy? (textbook, p. 162; video segments 5 and 6)

REVIEW

The following process is intended to help you retain the knowledge you have acquired in this lesson.

   a. Review the terms and concepts highlighted in the textbook.
   b. Review the checklists at the end of each section in the textbook.
   c. Review the Case in Point examples in the textbook.
   d. Review A Look Back in the textbook.
   e. Complete the following Practice Test and check your responses.
   f. Revisit the text and/or video for any questions you answer incorrectly on the Practice Test.

PRACTICE TEST

Multiple Choice: Circle the letter that corresponds to the BEST answer for each question.

1. Aggregate demand is the total value of real aggregate GDP that
   A. all sectors of the economy are willing to purchase at various price levels.
   B. all sectors of the economy are willing to purchase at various national income levels.
   C. consumers are willing to purchase at various price levels.
   D. consumers are willing to purchase at various national income levels.
   E. all sectors of the economy are willing to sell at various price levels.

2. The relationship between the total output produced and the price level, all other things unchanged, is
   A. market supply.
   B. surplus supply.
   C. national supply.
   D. excess supply.
   E. aggregate supply.

3. The economy's natural real output corresponds to the level of
   A. natural employment.
   B. frictional unemployment.
   C. structural unemployment.
   D. natural price level.
   E. average prices.

4. A recessionary gap occurs if
   A. actual real GDP is less than the natural level of real GDP.
   B. actual real GDP is greater than the natural level of real GDP.
   C. actual real GDP is equal to the natural level of real GDP.
   D. unemployment is less than the natural rate.
   E. unemployment is equal to the natural rate.

5. The short run in macroeconomic analysis is a period
   A. in which real wages are flexible.
   B. in which real wages are sticky.
   C. of less than one year.
   D. lasting between one and two years.
   E. lasting between two and five years.

6. When the economy is producing GDP above the natural level, it has
   A. a full-employment GDP.
   B. a natural level of employment.
   C. a recessionary gap.
   D. an inflationary gap.
   E. a long-run equilibrium condition.

---

7. An increase in aggregate demand is seen as
   A. a curvature of the aggregate demand curve.
   B. a downward movement along the aggregate demand curve.
   C. an upward movement along the aggregate demand curve.
   D. a shift to the left of the aggregate demand curve.
   E. a shift to the right of the aggregate demand curve.

8. A movement along the short-run aggregate supply curve in response to a change in the price level is called a
   A. determinant of aggregate supply.
   B. revealed cost on aggregate supply.
   C. rearrangement of economic production.
   D. change in aggregate supply.
   E. change in the aggregate quantity of goods and services supplied.

9. The downward-sloping aggregate demand curve suggests that
   A. people will buy fewer goods at higher prices than at lower prices.
   B. the public's real cash balances are larger at higher price levels than at lower price levels.
   C. the public's real cash balances are negative when the price level is rising.
   D. foreigners will buy more exported goods at higher domestic price levels.
   E. people will import more foreign goods at higher domestic price levels.

10. A decrease in aggregate supply will generate _____ in short-run real GDP and _____ in the price level.
    A. an increase; an increase
    B. an increase; a decrease
    C. a decrease; an increase
    D. a decrease; a decrease
    E. no change; no change

11. An increase in investment leads to _____ in the price level and _____ in real GDP.
    A. an increase; no change
    B. a decrease; no change
    C. no change; no change
    D. an increase; an increase
    E. a decrease; a decrease

12. An inflationary gap occurs if
    A. actual real GDP is less than natural real GDP.
    B. actual real GDP is greater than natural real GDP.
    C. actual real GDP is equal to natural real GDP.
    D. unemployment is greater than the natural rate.
    E. unemployment is equal to the natural rate.

13. When the economy is producing GDP below the natural level, it has
    A. a full-employment output.
    B. a natural level of employment.
    C. a recessionary gap.
    D. an inflationary gap.
    E. an equilibrium condition.

14. A recessionary gap is automatically closed by _____ wages that shift the _____.
    A. lower; SRAS curve to the right
    B. lower; LRAS curve to the right
    C. lower; SRAS curve to the left
    D. higher; SRAS curve to the right
    E. higher; SRAS curve to the left

15. A policy of intervention, aimed at shifting the aggregate demand curve in an effort to close a recessionary or an inflationary gap, is
    A. a welfare policy.
    B. a noninterventionist policy.
    C. an intermediate policy.
    D. a stabilization policy.
    E. an advanced policy.

16. A policy that allows the economy to close a recessionary or an inflationary gap through self-correction is
    A. a welfare policy.
    B. a noninterventionist policy.
    C. an intermediate policy.
    D. a stabilization policy.
    E. an advanced policy.

17. A decrease in aggregate demand will generate _____ in short-run real GDP and _____ in the price level.
    A. an increase; no change
    B. a decrease; no change
    C. a decrease; a decrease
    D. no change; an increase
    E. no change; a decrease

18. A decrease in raw materials costs leads to _____ in the price level and _____ in real GDP.
    A. an increase; a decrease
    B. a decrease; an increase
    C. an increase; no change
    D. a decrease; no change
    E. no change; no change

Shifts of the AD/SRAS Curves

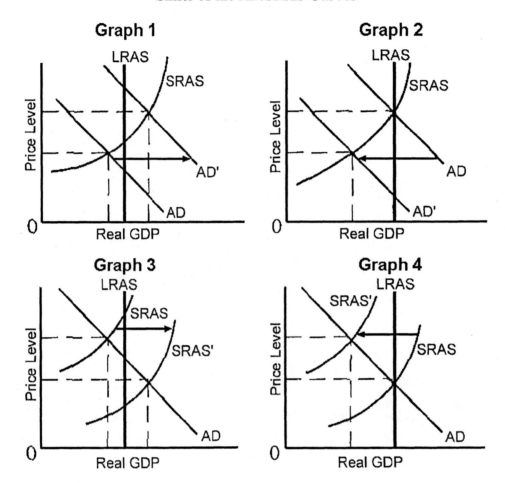

Use the graphs above to answer the following three questions.

19. Which graph(s) depicts the creation of a recessionary gap?
    A. Graph 1   D. All of the above
    B. Graph 2   E. None of the above
    C. Graph 3

20. Which graph(s) depicts the creation of an inflationary gap?
    A. Graph 1   D. Graph 4
    B. Graph 2   E. Graphs 1 and 3
    C. Graph 3

21. Which graph depicts the creation of stagflation?
    A. Graph 1   D. Graph 4
    B. Graph 2   E. None of the above
    C. Graph 3

Short-answer essay questions.

22. Explain how "sticky" prices may prevent markets or an economy from achieving equilibrium.

23. In the video "Aggregate Supply and Demand," what is an example of fiscal policy? How does fiscal policy differ from monetary policy?

24. What is expansionary policy?

25. What is contractionary policy?

ANSWER KEY

1. A ....LO 1 .... Tregarthen/Rittenberg, p. 145; video segment 2
2. E ....LO 1 .... Tregarthen/Rittenberg, p. 153; video segment 2
3. A ....LO 1 .... Tregarthen/Rittenberg, p. 152; video segment 2
4. A ....LO 1 .... Tregarthen/Rittenberg, p. 158; video segment 4
5. B ....LO 1 .... Tregarthen/Rittenberg, pp. 151–152; video segment 2
6. D ....LO 1, 8 ..... Tregarthen/Rittenberg, pp. 158–159; video segment 3
7. E ....LO 2 .... Tregarthen/Rittenberg, pp. 147–152; video segment 2
8. E ....LO 2 .... Tregarthen/Rittenberg, p. 147; video segment 2
9. E ....LO 3 .... Tregarthen/Rittenberg, p. 147; video segment 2
10. C ....LO 4 .... Tregarthen/Rittenberg, pp. 153–154; video segment 2
11. D ....LO 5 .... Tregarthen/Rittenberg, p. 148
12. B ....LO 1, 8 ..... Tregarthen/Rittenberg, pp. 158–159; video segment 3
13. C ....LO 1, 7 ..... Tregarthen/Rittenberg, pp. 158–159; video segment 4
14. A ....LO 10 .... Tregarthen/Rittenberg, p. 159; video segment 3
15. D ....LO 14 .... Tregarthen/Rittenberg, p. 160; video segment 5
16. B ....LO 14 .... Tregarthen/Rittenberg, p. 160; video segment 6
17. C ....LO 5 .... Tregarthen/Rittenberg, p. 148
18. B ....LO 4 .... Tregarthen/Rittenberg, pp. 153–154; video segment 2
19. B ....LO 7 .... Tregarthen/Rittenberg, p. 158; video segment 4
20. E ....LO 8 .... Tregarthen/Rittenberg, p. 158; video segment 3
21. D ....LO 9 .... Wyatt, telecourse guide Lesson 6 Overview

Short-answer essay questions.

22. LO 6 .... Tregarthen/Rittenberg, pp. 151–155
Since wages are often fixed in the short run due to contracts or other employment agreements and prices tend to change slowly, changes in market demand or market supply will cause shortages or surpluses that may persist. The "stickiness" of wages and prices will keep markets from achieving equilibrium.

23. LO 11 .... Tregarthen/Rittenberg, pp. 161–162; video segment 5
In the video "Aggregate Supply and Demand," government spending on programs to reduce poverty and defense spending during the Vietnam War are both examples of fiscal policy. Professor Mason cited the need for a contraction of the money supply and increases in interest rates to slow the inflation of this time period. Altering the money supply and interest rates represents monetary policy.

24. LO 12 .... Tregarthen/Rittenberg, pp. 160–162; video segment 5
Expansionary policy is aimed at increasing output production and employment, which reduces recessionary problems. Increases in government spending and/or decreases in taxes are expansionary fiscal policy. Increasing the money supply and/or decreasing interest rates is expansionary monetary policy. Expansionary policies cause an increase in the aggregate demand curve.

25. LO 13 .... Tregarthen/Rittenberg, pp. 160–162; video segment 5
Contractionary policy is aimed at decreasing output production and employment, which reduces inflationary problems. Decreases in government spending and/or increases in taxes are contractionary fiscal policy. Decreasing the money supply and/or increasing interest rates is contractionary monetary policy. Contractionary policies cause a decrease in the aggregate demand curve.

LESSON INTERVIEWEES

Kari L. Battaglia, Lecturer, Department of Economics, University of North Texas, Denton, TX

Teresa Ghilarducci, Economist, University of Notre Dame, Notre Dame, IN

Thomas J. Hern, Chair, Automotive Marketing Department, Northwood University, Cedar Hill, TX

Dr. Magnus L. Kpakol, Business Economist and Adjunct Professor of Economics, University of North Texas and University of Dallas, Denton and Irving, TX

Patrick Mason, Professor of Economics, Florida State University, Tallahassee, FL

Lesson 7

Economic Growth

OVERVIEW

Most societies have a goal of achieving consistent economic growth. Ideally, the economy will grow or expand at a faster rate than the population expands, which usually translates into an increase in the standard of living. Achieving economic growth has many obstacles. In addition to changing economic forces, social and political factors often present major barriers.

Segment 2 examines the factors of growth by highlighting the major economic achievements of Japan since World War II. One area in which Japan has excelled is the formation of capital. Capital formation is very important for an economy to grow; however, this requires sacrifices in terms of goods and services. If resources are used to produce capital or increase the quality of capital, including human capital, then the resources cannot be used to produce goods and services for current consumption. The rate of savings in an economy is also a very important factor; this determines the available funds for investment in capital production. It is important to note that people may or may not be willing to give up current consumption in exchange for potential increases in consumption in the future. Another important influence on economic growth in Japan has been the emphasis on education.

Segment 3 provides a contrast to the economic growth seen in Japan. It focuses on some of the countries of the former Soviet Union and their attempt to achieve growth in a very unstable economic situation. Most of the former Soviet countries are trying to create market-based economies. The video highlights how problems created by ethnic conflicts and the destruction of productive resources interfere with achieving this goal. The Soviet Union experienced massive growth since its creation in the early 1900s; however, the costs were extreme in terms of the sacrifices the population was forced to make in order to achieve these high rates of growth. Millions of people died due to resources being used for capital formation rather than producing food and shelter.

Segment 4 focuses on the problems that developing countries must overcome in order to grow and prosper. Excessive population, inadequate infrastructure, a high level of inequality in income distribution, and agrarian-based economies are some of the problems developing countries must face. These enormous obstacles may require internationally backed assistance to overcome them. The World Bank and the International Monetary Fund (IMF) are two institutions created in 1944 for this purpose. The goals of both institutions are to assist developing countries; however, their methods differ. There is not universal agreement on how to help these countries increase their standard of living.

LESSON ASSIGNMENTS

Text: Tregarthen and Rittenberg: *Macroeconomics*, Chapter 8, "Economic Growth," pp. 168–183, and Chapter 19, "Economic Development," pp. 394–414.

Video: "Economic Growth" from the series *Choices & Change: Macroeconomics*.

LESSON OBJECTIVES

1. Use an AS/AD graph to illustrate economic growth.

2. List the factors that affect the level of economic growth.

3. Explain the relationship between economic growth and the standard of living.

4. Explain the challenges faced by many developing countries striving for economic growth.

5. Discuss the pros and cons of government aid to developing countries.

6. Explain the challenges related to an economy changing from a command system to a market system.

LESSON FOCUS POINTS

The following questions are designed to help you get the most benefit from the resources selected for this lesson. To maximize your learning experience:

   a.   Scan the focus point questions.
   b.   Read the assigned text pages.
   c.   View the video.
   d.   Write answers to the following questions. (References in parentheses can be used to locate information in the text and video that will help you answer the question.)

1. Graphically illustrate the history of Japan since 1944 with AS/AD curves. (textbook, pp. 174–179; video segment 2)

2. Why is economic growth desirable? Based on the video "Economic Growth," list the reasons for Japan's recovery after WWII. (textbook, p. 168; video segment 2)

3. Economic growth implies a shift of the long-run aggregate supply curve to the right. How does economic growth relate to the standard of living? (textbook, pp. 168–172; video segment 1)

4. Based on the video "Economic Growth," explain some of the problems Russia is experiencing in transforming its economic system. (video segment 3)

5. What are the main differences between the World Bank and the International Monetary Fund? (video segment 4)

6. What are the characteristics of low-income countries? What are the challenges faced by developing countries trying to achieve higher standards of living? (textbook, pp. 396–398; video segment 4)

7. What are some of the criticisms of the World Bank and IMF policies for developing countries? (video segment 4)

REVIEW

The following process is intended to help you retain the knowledge you have acquired in this lesson.

a. Review the terms and concepts highlighted in the textbook.
b. Review the checklists at the end of each section in the textbook.
c. Review the Case in Point examples in the textbook.
d. Review A Look Back in the textbook.
e. Complete the following Practice Test and check your responses.
f. Revisit the text and/or video for any questions you answer incorrectly on the Practice Test.

PRACTICE TEST

Multiple Choice: Circle the letter that corresponds to the BEST answer for each question.

1. Economic growth is the
   A. efficiency with which an input is converted to an output.
   B. process through which increasingly larger quantities of inputs are needed to produce a given quantity of output.
   C. process through which the economy's natural level of real GDP is increased.
   D. difference between actual real GDP and potential real GDP.
   E. amount of aggregate output that is available at various price levels.

2. Economic growth is most closely related to
   A. business cycles.
   B. long-term changes in the standard of living.
   C. short-term changes in the standard of living.
   D. day-to-day changes in business activity.
   E. quarter-to-quarter changes in business activity.

Economic Growth

Country	F	G	H	I	J
Population	100	10	40	50	60
Nominal GDP	$100,000	$15,000	$8,000	$80,000	$36,000
Price level	10	3	1	4	2

Use the table above to answer the following two questions.

3. Per capita real GDP in country I is
   A. $100.
   B. $200.
   C. $300.
   D. $400.
   E. $500.

4. The country with the highest level of per capita real GDP is country
   A. F.
   B. G.
   C. H.
   D. I.
   E. J.

5. A source of economic growth brought about by technological change is the
   A. invention of the automobile.
   B. discovery of petroleum reserves in Alaska.
   C. increase in the population from 1900 to 1990.
   D. increase in the number of women in the labor force.
   E. increase in the number of teenagers in the labor force.

6. In general, an economy that saves more today will
   A. show an increase in consumption today.
   B. show a decrease in consumption in the future.
   C. be able to produce less real output in the future.
   D. be able to produce more real output in the future.
   E. cause the production possibilities curve to shift inward.

7. Compared to more developed countries, less developed countries are often characterized by
   A. lower rates of population growth.
   B. greater income inequality.
   C. a smaller share of income used for consumption.
   D. a smaller proportion of the labor force in agriculture.
   E. a greater diversity of products exported to other countries.

8. Compared to more developed countries, less developed countries are often characterized by
   A. lower rates of population growth.
   B. greater government control by large, relatively poor groups.
   C. inadequate health care facilities.
   D. a smaller proportion of the labor force in agriculture.
   E. a greater diversity of products exported to other countries.

9. Compared to more developed countries, less developed countries are often characterized by
   A. lower rates of population growth.
   B. greater government control by large, relatively poor groups.
   C. a smaller share of income used for consumption.
   D. a smaller proportion of the labor force in agriculture.
   E. a greater reliance on a few products exported to other countries.

10. The concept that poverty found in less developed countries is primarily caused by the inability of developing nations to free themselves from dependence on industrialized nations is the
    A. Solow growth model.
    B. demographic transition.
    C. rule of 72.
    D. dependency theory.
    E. marginal productivity theory.

11. The problems encountered by transitional economies trying to become well-functioning market economies involve
    A. eliminating bank checking accounts in favor of paper currency.
    B. taking steps to raise the inflation rate.
    C. expanding private property rights.
    D. eliminating all welfare programs and social safety nets.
    E. maintaining public perception that capitalism is evil.

Short-answer essay questions.

12. Graphically illustrate how economic growth is portrayed in the AS/AD model.

13. List the pros and cons of international aid to developing countries.

14. Why is Russia encountering major obstacles to market reform?

ANSWER KEY

1. C ....LO 1.......... Tregarthen/Rittenberg, p. 169; video segment 1
2. B ....LO 3.......... Tregarthen/Rittenberg, p. 169; video segment 1
3. D ....LO 3.......... Tregarthen/Rittenberg, p. 172
4. B ....LO 3.......... Tregarthen/Rittenberg, p. 172
5. A ....LO 2.......... Tregarthen/Rittenberg, p. 177–180; video segment 1
6. D ....LO 2.......... Tregarthen/Rittenberg, p. 179–182; video segment 2
7. B ....LO 4.......... Tregarthen/Rittenberg, pp. 396–398
8. C ....LO 4.......... Tregarthen/Rittenberg, pp. 396–398; video segment 4
9. E ....LO 4.......... Tregarthen/Rittenberg, pp. 396–398
10. D ....LO 5.......... Tregarthen/Rittenberg, p. 409
11. C ....LO 6.......... Tregarthen/Rittenberg, video segment 3

Short-answer essay questions.

12. LO 1 .... Tregarthen/Rittenberg, pp. 174–176; video segment 1

Economic growth is shown by a shift to the right of the long-run aggregate supply curve.

13. LO 5 .... Tregarthen/Rittenberg, pp. 407–412; video segment 4
The benefits of aid include reducing infant mortality rates; increasing access to potable water; and providing basic health services, sanitation improvements, and education.
The downside of aiding developing countries is inefficient distribution of aid and potential dependence on foreign aid.

14. LO 6 .... Tregarthen/Rittenberg, pp. 428–429; video segment 3
Most of the Russian population had only experienced the Soviet system; therefore, capitalism was a new experience. Their culture, based on socialism and negative attitudes towards capitalism, has made the transition difficult. Declining infrastructure, political instability, currency fluctuations, and lack of laws protecting businesses are other factors that make the transition difficult.

LESSON INTERVIEWEES

Keishiro Ariizumi, Student, Dallas Japanese Society, Dallas, TX

J. Michael Finger, Lead Economist, The World Bank, Washington, DC

Jo Marie Greisgraber, Project Director, Rethinking Bretton Woods, Center of Concern, Washington, DC

Yuki Hou, Student, Dallas Japanese Society, Dallas, TX

Jeffrey Minsky, Chief Financial Officer, Protek Flagship Ltd., Pittsburgh, PA

David Ramsour, President, Texas Council of Economic Education, Houston, TX

Jorge A. Sanguinetty, Chairman, CEO, and President, DevTech Systems, Washington, DC

Philip Seib, Political Analyst, WFAA-TV, Dallas, TX

Shohei Takamatsu, Owner, Royal Tokyo Restaurant, Dallas, TX

Nobuo Tani, Assistant General Manager, NEC America, Inc., Dallas, TX

Wanda Tseng, Deputy Director, International Monetary Fund, Washington, DC

Lesson 8

The Nature of Money

OVERVIEW

This is a lesson that students usually enjoy, because it involves learning about "money." The lesson starts with a brief history of money, including a myriad of things that have been used as money over the centuries. Most of the examples chosen had problems associated with using the items as money. For instance, it was difficult to carry around bales of cotton or make change with diamonds. In our modern-day economy, there are still many different forms of money. The measurement of the different forms of money is highlighted in the video as M1, M2, and M3.

The third segment presents the creation of the Federal Reserve (commonly referred to as "the Fed") by Congress in 1913. The Federal Reserve has many responsibilities with the most important one being to maintain the stability of our money supply.

The next segment is the most challenging part of the lesson because of the complexity of the money creation process. Printing additional dollars is NOT the primary means of altering the money supply. The Treasury Department's Bureau of Engraving and Printing is responsible for the printing of our paper currency. The Federal Reserve puts these dollars into circulation to replace worn-out currency and to supply additional reserves when needed. Money is primarily created through loan-making activity, which creates more deposits and additional reserves, which leads to additional loan-making activity, additional deposits, additional reserves and so on. There is a limit to the loan-making ability and, therefore, money creation, from a change in reserves (R). This can be calculated with the deposit multiplier (m_d). Additional excess reserves (ER) multiplied by the reciprocal of the required reserve ratio (rrr) is the maximum potential change in the money supply. Note: In the video, required reserve ratio is written as r.

The last segment focuses on the Federal Reserve's major responsibility of managing the money supply and the tools at its disposal to manipulate the money supply. The most frequently used tool of the Fed is open-market operations (OMO), the buying or selling of government securities. The Federal Open Market Committee (FOMC) determines the amount of securities that are bought or sold. It is important to note the Fed does not have complete control over the money supply. The behavior of banks and consumers can limit the Fed's ability to manipulate the economy through manipulation of the money supply. The Federal Reserve is a very powerful entity, and there is some disagreement about whether it should maintain its autonomy and power.

LESSON ASSIGNMENTS

Text: Tregarthen and Rittenberg: *Macroeconomics*, Chapter 9, "The Nature and Creation of Money," pp. 184–203.

Video: "The Nature of Money" from the series *Choices & Change: Macroeconomics.*

LESSON OBJECTIVES

1. Define money.

2. Explain the functions of money.

3. Distinguish between commodity money and fiat money.

4. Define liquidity.

5. Explain how each component of M1, M2, and M3 meets the definition of money and performs the functions of money.

6. Define financial intermediary.

7. Distinguish the different characteristics of financial intermediaries.

8. Explain a fractional reserve banking system.

9. Interpret a T-account to identify assets and liabilities.

10. Use T-accounts to illustrate how banks can create or destroy money.

11. Calculate the deposit multiplier.

12. Describe the structure of the Fed.

13. Describe the functions of the Fed.

14. Describe the major tools of the Fed for altering the money supply.

15. Explain the advantages and disadvantages of having the Fed largely independent of the federal government.

LESSON FOCUS POINTS

The following questions are designed to help you get the most benefit from the resources selected for this lesson. To maximize your learning experience:

a. Scan the focus point questions.
b. Read the assigned text pages.
c. View the video.
d. Write answers to the following questions. (References in parentheses can be used to locate information in the text and video that will help you answer the question.)

1. Choose three different items from the video "The Nature of Money" that have historically been used as a medium of exchange. Explain what makes each of these items less than desirable as a form of money. (video segment 2)

2. Briefly explain how currency performs the three functions of money. (textbook, pp. 184–185; video segment 2)

3. How does commodity money differ from fiat money? Provide an example of commodity money and an example of fiat money. (textbook, pp. 185–186; video segment 2)

4. Explain what is meant by the term *liquidity*? Provide an example of an asset that is considered to be highly liquid and one that is not. What is the most liquid of all assets? (textbook, p. 187; video segment 2)

5. Definitions of money vary depending on their liquidity. List the components of the money supply from the most liquid to the least liquid. Explain the differences among M1, M2, and M3. (textbook, p. 187; video segment 2)

6. What are the functions of a financial intermediary? List four types of financial intermediaries. (textbook, p. 189)

7. What are the major differences among the institutions you listed in the previous question? (textbook, p. 189)

8. The United States operates with a fractional reserve banking system. Briefly explain how this system works and list the benefits of the system. (textbook, p. 191; video segment 4)

9. Provide examples of assets and liabilities for a financial intermediary. Use a T-account to illustrate your examples. (textbook, pp. 190–191; video segment 4)

10. Assuming a required reserve ratio of 8 percent, use T-accounts to illustrate the money creation process initiated by an additional $10,000 of currency deposited into the banking system. Assume the following: (1) banks are currently fully loaned up, (2) banks choose to hold zero excess reserves (ER), and (3) there are no leakages into cash. Take the process through five loan creations. What would happen if the situation were reversed? (textbook, pp. 191–194; video segment 4)

11. Using the example in the previous question, what is the simple deposit multiplier? What is the maximum potential change in the money supply from the $10,000 deposit? (textbook, p. 193; video segment 4)

12. Describe the structure of the Federal Reserve by addressing the following: (textbook, pp. 196–197; video segment 3)
    A. What is our nation's central bank?
    B. How many district banks does our central bank have?
    C. How many members sit on the Board of Governors, how are they appointed, and how long do they serve?

D. What is the purpose of the Federal Open Market Committee (FOMC) and who serves on this committee?

E. Who owns the Federal Reserve District Banks?

F. Are they in operation to make a profit?

13. The Federal Reserve's primary responsibility is to manage the nation's money supply. Briefly explain the other services the Fed provides to financial institutions. (textbook, p. 196; video segment 3)

14. What are the three major tools of monetary policy? Briefly describe how each tool can change the money supply. (textbook, pp. 197–200; video segment 5)

15. In the video "The Nature of Money," what are the arguments for and against having an independent Federal Reserve System? (video segments 3 and 5)

REVIEW

The following process is intended to help you retain the knowledge you have acquired in this lesson.

a. Review the terms and concepts highlighted in the textbook.
b. Review the checklists at the end of each section in the textbook.
c. Review the Case in Point examples in the textbook.
d. Review A Look Back in the textbook.
e. Complete the following Practice Test and check your responses.
f. Revisit the text and/or video for any questions you answer incorrectly on the Practice Test.

PRACTICE TEST

Multiple Choice: Circle the letter that corresponds to the BEST answer for each question.

1. Money is anything that
   A. can be converted into gold with relatively little loss in value.
   B. can be converted into silver with relatively little loss in value.
   C. serves as a medium of exchange for goods and services.
   D. facilitates a connecting link between credit instruments and debt instruments.
   E. facilitates the wholesaling or retailing of funds.

2. Inflation of the general price level reduces the ability of money to function as a
   A. medium of exchange.
   B. medium of value.
   C. unit of account.
   D. standard of deferred payment.
   E. store of value.

3. The unit-of-account function means money is used
   A. as a consistent means of measuring the value of things.
   B. as the common denominator of future payments.
   C. to pay for goods and services.
   D. to accumulate purchasing power.
   E. to facilitate a double coincidence of wants.

4. Money that has value apart from its use as money is
   A. fiat money.
   B. currency.
   C. convertible paper money.
   D. private debt money.
   E. commodity money.

5. The ease in which an asset can be exchanged for currency represents
   A. M3.
   B. reserves.
   C. liabilities.
   D. liquidity.
   E. M2.

6. The largest component of M1 is
   A. currency.
   B. coin.
   C. checkable deposits.
   D. savings deposits.
   E. time deposits.

7. A classification of money that is included in M3 but not in M2 is
   A. currency.
   B. demand deposits.
   C. banker's acceptances.
   D. small-denomination time deposits.
   E. large-denomination time deposits.

8. An institution that collects funds from lenders and distributes these funds to borrowers is
   A. a financial intermediary.
   B. the Federal Reserve System.
   C. a wholesale store.
   D. a retail store.
   E. the Federal Deposit Insurance Corporation.

9. The principle of fractional reserve banking makes it possible for a
   A. bank to make loans.
   B. bank to print currency.
   C. bank to avoid reserve requirements.
   D. goldsmith to print currency.
   E. goldsmith to establish the gold standard.

Components of the Money System
(in billions of dollars)

Currency	$100
Checkable deposits	300
Traveler's checks	50
Small-denomination time deposits	700
Savings deposits	75
Money market mutual funds (individuals)	500
Other liquid assets	150
Large-denomination time deposits	200
Money market mutual funds (institutions)	125
Other less liquid assets	125

Use the table above to answer the following two questions.

10. The money supply measured by M2 is
   A. $450 billion.
   B. $1,425 billion.
   C. $1,875 billion.
   D. $2,200 billion.
   E. $2,550 billion.

11. The difference between M1 and M2 is
   A. $325 billion.
   B. $350 billion.
   C. $450 billion.
   D. $1,425 billion.
   E. $1,875 billion.

12. The law requires banks to maintain
   A. fractional reserves in the form of deposit liabilities against their liquid assets.
   B. fractional reserves in the form of federal securities against their outstanding loans.
   C. fractional reserves in the form of liquid assets against their deposit liabilities.
   D. legal reserves in the form of gold against their outstanding loans.
   E. legal reserves equal to their net worth.

13. Which of the following are bank reserves?
   A. Demand deposits with other banks
   B. Deposits with the Federal Reserve
   C. Treasury bonds and bills
   D. State bonds of the state in which the bank is located but not state bonds of other states
   E. State bonds of any and all states in the United States

14. A bank is fully loaned up when
    A. legal reserves are zero.
    B. excess reserves are zero.
    C. primary reserves are zero.
    D. required reserves are zero.
    E. nonlegal reserves are zero.

15. Assume that all banks in the banking system are fully loaned up and that the required reserve ratio is 20 percent. If one bank obtains excess reserves of $10,000, then checkable deposits could ultimately increase by
    A. $10,000.
    B. $20,000.
    C. $30,000.
    D. $40,000.
    E. $50,000.

16. To reduce the political influence of the Board of Governors,
    A. the president appoints a new board every 4 years.
    B. the president appoints a new board every 8 years.
    C. the reelection campaign for each member is less than 1 year.
    D. each member is appointed for 7 years, with one term expiring every year.
    E. each member is appointed for 14 years.

17. A primary function of a central bank is to
    A. regulate dividend payments by corporations.
    B. control the bond market.
    C. set monetary policy.
    D. publish statistics on banking and related financial matters.
    E. determine the international balance of payments.

18. Federal Reserve Banks are owned by
    A. their member banks.
    B. Wall Street investors.
    C. the Board of Governors.
    D. the U.S. Treasury.
    E. the Bank of the United States.

19. Assume that the banking system has $10,000 in deposits and $1,000 in reserves. If the required reserve ratio changes from 10 percent to 5 percent
    A. reserves will decrease to $500.
    B. excess reserves will increase to $500.
    C. required reserves will increase to $1,000.
    D. total deposits in the banking system will ultimately decline.
    E. banks must transfer $500 of nonlegal reserves into legal reserves.

20. The most important tool of monetary policy for achieving economic stabilization is
    A. moral suasion.
    B. reserve ratios.
    C. the discount rate.
    D. margin requirements.
    E. open-market operations.

Short-answer essay questions.

21. List three different types of financial intermediaries and their characteristics.

22. Draw a T-account and place three different types of assets and three different types of liabilities for a commercial bank in the T-account.

23. Use T-accounts to illustrate money creation from an increase in excess reserves of $20,000 with a required reserve ratio of 10 percent.

24. What is the potential maximum increase in the money supply from the previous question?

25. List the major functions of the Federal Reserve Banks.

26. Do you think the Federal Reserve Banks should retain their autonomous standing? Why?

ANSWER KEY

 1. C .... LO 1 .... Tregarthen/Rittenberg, p. 184; video segment 2
 2. E .... LO 2 .... Tregarthen/Rittenberg, p. 185; video segment 2
 3. A .... LO 2 .... Tregarthen/Rittenberg, p. 185; video segment 2
 4. E .... LO 3 .... Tregarthen/Rittenberg, p. 185; video segment 2
 5. D .... LO 4 .... Tregarthen/Rittenberg, p. 187; video segment 2
 6. C .... LO 5 .... Tregarthen/Rittenberg, pp. 187–188; video segment 2
 7. E .... LO 5 .... video segment 2
 8. A .... LO 6 .... Tregarthen/Rittenberg, p. 189; video segment 4
 9. A .... LO 8 .... Tregarthen/Rittenberg, pp. 190–191; video segment 4
10. C .... LO 5 .... Tregarthen/Rittenberg, p. 187; video segment 2
11. D .... LO 5 .... Tregarthen/Rittenberg, p. 187; video segment 2
12. C .... LO 8 .... Tregarthen/Rittenberg, pp. 190–191; video segment 4
13. B .... LO 8 .... Tregarthen/Rittenberg, pp. 190–191; video segment 4
14. B .... LO 8 .... Tregarthen/Rittenberg, p. 191; video segment 4
15. E .... LO 11 .... Tregarthen/Rittenberg, pp. 193–194; video segment 4
16. E .... LO 12 .... Tregarthen/Rittenberg, p. 197; video segment 4
17. C .... LO 13 .... Tregarthen/Rittenberg, p. 197; video segment 3
18. A .... LO 12 .... Tregarthen/Rittenberg, p. 196; video segment 3
19. B .... LO 14 .... Tregarthen/Rittenberg, p. 191; video segment 4
20. E .... LO 14 .... Tregarthen/Rittenberg, p. 198; video segment 5

Short-answer essay questions.

21. LO 7 .... Tregarthen/Rittenberg, p. 189
Financial intermediaries accept deposits from certain groups and offer loans to others. The most important intermediaries are commercial banks. The main characteristic that sets banks apart from other intermediaries is that they are allowed to offer checkable deposits. Insurance companies and pension funds are also financial intermediaries; however, they do not offer checking accounts.

22. LO 9 .... Tregarthen/Rittenberg, pp. 189–194; video segment 4

Assets	Liabilities
Reserves	Checkable deposits
Loans	Other deposits
Bonds	Loans

23. LO 10 .... Tregarthen/Rittenberg, pp. 191–194; video segment 4

Bank A

Assets		Liabilities
Reserves (ER	+20,000 18,000)	+20,000 deposit
Reserves	2,000	
Loans	18,000	

Bank B

Assets		Liabilities
Reserves (ER	+18,000 16,200)	+18,000 deposit
Reserves	1,800	
Loans	16,200	

Bank C

Assets		Liabilities
Reserves (ER	+16,200 14,580)	+16,200 deposit
Reserves	1,620	
Loans	14,580	

Bank D

Assets		Liabilities
Reserves (ER	+14,580 13,122)	+14,580 deposit
Reserves	1,458	
Loans	13,122	

If we assume that banks wish to hold no excess reserves, then the loan-making activity will continue as long as there are excess reserves (ER).

24. LO 10, 11 .... Tregarthen/Rittenberg, pp. 193–194; video segment 4
The maximum potential change in the money supply is found by multiplying (ER) times the simple deposit multiplier (1/rrr).

$$ER(1/rrr) =$$

$$18,000 \ (1/.10) = \$180,000$$

25. LO 13 .... Tregarthen/Rittenberg, p. 196; video segment 3
In addition to their main function of maintaining the stability of the money supply, the Federal Reserve Banks also:
A. provide check clearing services.
B. act as fiscal agents for the U.S. Treasury.
C. are lenders of last resort.
D. are bank regulators.

26. LO 15 .... Tregarthen/Rittenberg, pp. 196–200; video segments 3 and 5
The answer to this question is based on your opinions. Make sure you have included the basis for your opinion.

LESSON INTERVIEWEES

Jeff Carbiener, Adjunct Professor of Economics, Southern Methodist University, Dallas, TX
Stan Carnes, Managing Director, Salomon Smith Barney, New York City, NY
Howard Hamilton, Executive Vice-President, McIlroy Bank and Trust Company, Fayetteville, AR
Steve Malin, Assistant Vice-President, Media Relations Officer and Senior Economist, Federal Reserve Bank of New York, New York, NY
Duane Rosa, Professor of Economics, West Texas A&M University, Canyon, TX
Philip Seib, Political Analyst, WFAA-TV, Dallas, TX
Ed Stevens, Senior Consultant and Economist, Federal Reserve Bank of Cleveland, Cleveland, OH

Lesson 9

Financial Markets

OVERVIEW

This lesson brings financial markets into the picture. Interest rates, bond prices, currency exchange rates, and other financial aspects directly and indirectly affect the macroeconomy. U.S. government bonds and the inverse relationship that exists between bond prices and interest rates are presented. U.S. bonds are generally considered to be "risk free," which explains the lower yields on these instruments. Just how risk free these securities are was questioned in 1995 when the government ran out of funds and had an interest payment due. This created the possibility of default; however, the markets did not show much reaction. The government shut down nonessential activities for approximately three weeks, the interest payment was made, and life went back to normal. When the market for bonds is in motion, supply and demand analysis is useful in analyzing the price changes. Price changes in turn change the yields or interest on these bonds. This segment also addresses the international effects of changes in the bond markets.

The third segment focuses on currency markets. The demand for U.S. government bonds by foreigners is related to the demand for U.S. dollars. Again supply and demand analysis is used to examine how changes in the market cause changes in currency prices. Governments sometimes take actions that directly affect currency markets and prices. This segment also illustrates why there is a demand for foreign currencies. For example, importing and exporting usually require currency exchange; tourism and investors seeking out the best return versus risk may need foreign currency to buy foreign bonds. The introduction of the Euro is also explored in this segment.

The next segment illustrates how financial markets cause changes in interest rates, which cause changes in spending, which then cause changes in aggregate demand. Changes in interest rates have a double effect on aggregate demand. Not only does business investment change due to interest rate changes, but consumer spending that depends on interest rates also changes.

How bond markets, currency markets, and money markets are interrelated and how they affect the macroeconomy are the focuses of the last part of this video.

LESSON ASSIGNMENTS

Text: Tregarthen and Rittenberg: *Macroeconomics*, Chapter 10, "Financial Markets and the Economy," pp. 204–222.

Video: "Financial Markets" from the series *Choices & Change: Macroeconomics*.

LESSON OBJECTIVES

1. Distinguish between the face value and the price of a bond.

2. Explain the inverse relationship between interest rates and bond prices.

3. Calculate the yield on a bond.

4. Explain why an increase in bond prices might result in an increase in aggregate demand and vice versa.

5. Explain why foreigners might want domestic currency and why locals might want foreign currency.

6. Explain how a change in the interest rate of a country might affect the demand for its currency.

7. Explain how a change in the exchange rate or in interest rates might affect aggregate demand.

8. Describe the factors that affect how much money people wish to hold.

9. Explain the graph of money supply.

10. Define money market equilibrium.

11. Explain what causes movement toward equilibrium when the actual interest rate is above or below its equilibrium level.

12. Interpret graphs of aggregate supply and demand that display the effects of changes in the money supply.

LESSON FOCUS POINTS

The following questions are designed to help you get the most benefit from the resources selected for this lesson. To maximize your learning experience:

    a.   Scan the focus point questions.
    b.   Read the assigned text pages.
    c.   View the video.
    d.   Write answers to the following questions. (References in parentheses can be used to locate information in the text and video that will help you answer the question.)

1. What is the difference between the face value and the price of a bond? When are they the same? (textbook, p. 205)

2. What causes bond prices to change? Explain why interest rates go down when bond prices rise and why bond prices fall when interest rates go up. (textbook, p. 205; video segment 2)

3. Calculate the yield on a $100,000 bond if you pay $85,000 for the bond. (textbook, p. 205)

4. Briefly explain how a change in bond prices affects investment and aggregate demand. Explain the process for both an increase and a decrease in bond prices. (textbook, pp. 206–207; video segment 2)

5. Why are there currency markets? Who are the suppliers and who are the demanders of currencies? (textbook, pp. 207–208; video segment 3)

6. Financial capital will flow to where it can get the highest return for a given level of risk. If interest rates are higher in the United States than in Japan, what will holders of financial capital in Japan do? Will this situation increase or decrease the demand for U.S. dollars? How will this example affect currency markets? (textbook, pp. 207–210; video segment 3)

7. Using supply and demand analysis, what are two ways the dollar can appreciate (increase in value)? What effect will an appreciating dollar have on the volume of imports and exports and therefore aggregate demand? Using supply and demand analysis, what are two ways the dollar can depreciate (decrease in value)? What effect will a depreciating dollar have on the volume of imports and exports and therefore aggregate demand? (textbook, pp. 208–210; video segment 3)

8. Define the demand for money. What factors affect the quantities of money people choose to hold? (textbook, p. 211; video segment 4)

9. Construct a graph of the money supply. Briefly explain the shape of the money supply curve. What factors cause this curve to shift? (textbook, pp. 215–216; video segment 4)

10. Graphically illustrate and explain money market equilibrium. (textbook, pp. 217–218; video segment 4)

11. When interest rates are above the money market equilibrium interest rate, what will happen to move interest rates toward equilibrium? When interest rates are below the money market equilibrium interest rate, what will happen to move interest rates toward equilibrium? (textbook, pp. 212–213; video segments 4 and 5)

12. Using the AS/AD model, graphically illustrate and then explain how changes in the money supply affect interest rates and, subsequently, aggregate demand. (textbook, pp. 216–218; video segment 4)

REVIEW

The following process is intended to help you retain the knowledge you have acquired in this lesson.

a. Review the terms and concepts highlighted in the textbook.
b. Review the checklists at the end of each section in the textbook.
c. Review the Case in Point examples in the textbook.
d. Review A Look Back in the textbook.
e. Complete the following Practice Test and check your responses.
f. Revisit the text and/or video for any questions you answer incorrectly on the Practice Test.

PRACTICE TEST

Multiple Choice: Circle the letter that corresponds to the BEST answer for each question.

The Bond Market

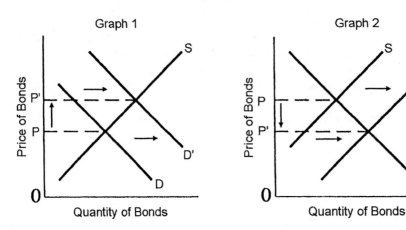

Graph 1   Graph 2

Use the graphs above to answer the following two questions.

1. Given the bond market illustrated in Graph 1, the interest rate will
   A. increase.
   B. decrease.
   C. remain unchanged.
   D. increase then return to the original level.
   E. decrease then return to the original level.

2. Given the bond market illustrated in Graph 2, the interest rate will _____ and business investment will _____.
   A. increase; increase
   B. increase; decrease
   C. decrease; increase
   D. decrease; decrease
   E. increase; remain unchanged

3. The amount that will be paid to the holder of a bond when it matures is its
   A. stock price.
   B. yield.
   C. interest rate.
   D. market value.
   E. face value.

4. An increase in the demand for bonds generates _____ in the interest rate and _____ in aggregate demand.
   A. an increase; an increase
   B. an increase; a decrease
   C. a decrease; an increase
   D. a decrease; a decrease
   E. no change; no change

5. A decrease in the demand for bonds generates _____ in the interest rate and _____ in the exchange rate.
   A. an increase; an increase
   B. an increase; a decrease
   C. a decrease; an increase
   D. a decrease; a decrease
   E. no change; no change

6. If the U.S. exchange rate increases relative to currencies in other countries, then United States
   A. imports and exports will both increase.
   B. imports and exports will both decrease.
   C. imports will decrease and exports will increase.
   D. imports will increase and exports will decrease.
   E. imports and exports will not change.

7. The money households and firms hold in order to pay for the goods and services they buy is the
   A. velocity demand.
   B. precautionary demand.
   C. transactions demand.
   D. transfer demand.
   E. speculative demand.

8. The money households and firms hold because of a concern that bond prices and the prices of other financial assets might fall is the
   A. velocity demand.
   B. precautionary demand.
   C. transactions demand.
   D. transfer demand.
   E. speculative demand.

9. The slope of the supply curve of money is
   A. vertical.
   B. horizontal.
   C. zero.
   D. negative.
   E. U-shaped.

Monetary Policy and the AD-SRAS Model

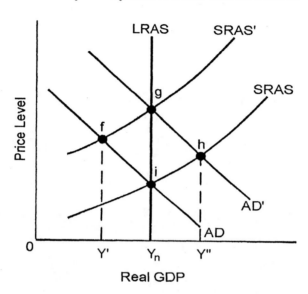

Use the graph above to answer the following question.

10. An increase in the money supply is most likely to cause a shift
    A. from SRAS to SRAS'.
    B. from AD to AD'.
    C. from SRAS' to SRAS.
    D. from AD' to AD.
    E. of the LRAS curve.

11. The interaction among institutions through which money is supplied to individuals, firms, and other institutions that demand money is the
    A. transfer market.
    B. velocity of money market.
    C. exchange market.
    D. currency market.
    E. money market.

12. Money market equilibrium occurs at the interest rate at which the
    A. quantity of money demanded is equal to the quantity of money supplied.
    B. quantity of money demanded is less than the quantity of money supplied.
    C. quantity of money demanded is greater than the quantity of money supplied.
    D. slopes of the demand curve for money and the supply curve for money are equal.
    E. demand curve for money and the supply curve for money are tangent.

13. An increase in the supply of money, with no change in the demand for money, will lead to _____ in equilibrium quantity of money and _____ in equilibrium interest rate.
   A. an increase; an increase
   B. an increase; a decrease
   C. a decrease; an increase
   D. a decrease; a decrease
   E. no change; no change

14. An increase in the supply of money will lead to _____ in equilibrium real GDP and _____ in equilibrium interest rate.
   A. an increase; an increase
   B. an increase; a decrease
   C. a decrease; an increase
   D. a decrease; a decrease
   E. no change; no change

Economic Adjustments

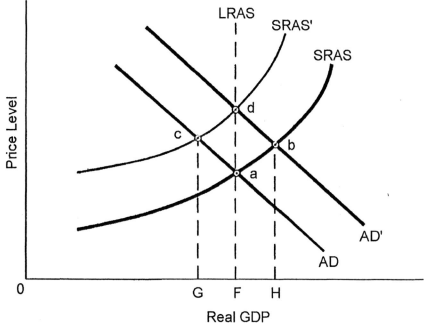

Use the graph above to answer the following question.

15. Assume that the economy is at point b. A decrease in the money supply would cause
   A. a shift of the SRAS curve to SRAS'.
   B. a shift of the SRAS' curve to SRAS.
   C. a shift of the AD curve to AD'.
   D. a shift of the AD' curve to AD.
   E. no change in the AD or SRAS curves.

Short-answer essay questions.

16. If the face value on a bond is $100,000 and the market price is $90,000, what is the interest rate? What happens to the interest rate when the price rises to $92,000?

17. Based on the video "Financial Markets," what stimulates the demand for foreign currency?

18. Graphically illustrate and explain how the money market seeks equilibrium.

ANSWER KEY

1. B ....LO 2.......... Tregarthen/Rittenberg, p. 205; video segment 2
2. B ....LO 2, 4...... Tregarthen/Rittenberg, p. 205; video segment 2
3. E ....LO 1.......... Tregarthen/Rittenberg, p. 205
4. C ....LO 4.......... Tregarthen/Rittenberg, pp. 206–207; video segment 2
5. A ....LO 2, 5, 6.. Tregarthen/Rittenberg, pp. 207–210; video segment 3
6. D ....LO 7.......... Tregarthen/Rittenberg, p. 210; video segments 3 and 4
7. C ....LO 8.......... Tregarthen/Rittenberg, p. 211
8. E ....LO 8.......... Tregarthen/Rittenberg, p. 211
9. A ....LO 9.......... Tregarthen/Rittenberg, pp. 215–216; video segments 3 and 4
10. B ....LO 12....... Tregarthen/Rittenberg, pp. 216–219; video segment 4
11. E ....LO 10....... Tregarthen/Rittenberg, p. 216
12. A ....LO 10....... Tregarthen/Rittenberg, p. 216; video segment 4
13. B ....LO 10, 11.. Tregarthen/Rittenberg, pp. 216–219; video segment 4
14. B ....LO 12....... Tregarthen/Rittenberg, pp. 216–219; video segment 4
15. D ....LO 12....... Tregarthen/Rittenberg, pp. 217–218; video segment 4

Short-answer essay questions.

16. LO 1, 2, 3............... Tregarthen/Rittenberg, p. 205

$$(100,000 - 90,000) / 90,000$$

$$10,000 / 90,000 = 0.11 = 11\%$$

$$(100,000 - 92,000) / 92,000$$

$$8,000 / 92,000 = 0.087 = 8.7\%$$

As bond prices rise, interest rates fall.

17. LO 5, 6.................... Tregarthen/Rittenberg, pp. 207–210; video segment 3
In the video "Financial Markets," there are several reasons for demanding foreign currency.
   A. Financial investment flows to the highest interest rates per a given level of risk. If that is in a foreign country, that currency is needed to buy those bonds.
   B. Tourists require foreign currencies.
   C. Importers and exporters have a need for currency markets.

18. LO 11 .... Tregarthen/Rittenberg, pp. 209–210; video segment 3

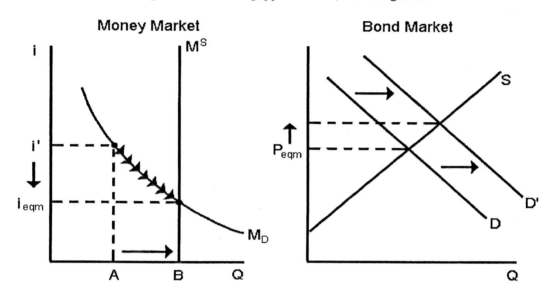

If interest rates are i', then the quantity demanded of money (A) is less than the quantity supplied (B). Because of higher interest rates, money flows into bonds, increasing the demand for bonds. This demand increase drives up the price of bonds and decreases market interest rates. This activity will continue, *ceteris paribus*, as long as market interest rates exceed equilibrium interest rates.

LESSON INTERVIEWEES

Kari Battaglia, Lecturer, Department of Economics, University of North Texas, Denton, TX

Sam F. Ciccarello, General Manager, Vigo Importing Company, Tampa, FL

George Friedlander, Managing Director—Fixed Income Strategist, Salomon Smith Barney, New York City, NY

William C. Gruben, Chief International Economist, Federal Reserve Bank of Dallas, Dallas, TX

David Johnson, Stockbroker, Dallas, TX

James A. Kornegay Jr., Tourist, Allen, TX

Dr. Magnus L. Kpakol, Business Economist and Adjunct Professor of Economics, University of North Texas, Denton, TX and University of Dallas, Irving, TX

Steve Malin, Assistant Vice-President, Media Relations Officer and Senior Economist, Federal Reserve Bank of New York, New York, NY

Robert D. McTeer Jr., President and CEO, Federal Reserve Bank of Dallas, Dallas, TX

Louis Richard, Sector Manager, Cargill, Inc., Tampa, FL

Philip Seib, Political Analyst, WFAA-TV, Dallas, TX

Lesson 10

Monetary Policy

OVERVIEW

Now that you have learned about money creation and the structure of the Federal Reserve System, it is time to look at the Fed's use of discretionary monetary policy to influence the macroeconomy. Recall the tools available for the Fed's use in stabilizing the economy: open-market operations, the discount rate, and the reserve ratio. This lesson focuses on how these tools can alter the macroeconomy and on the problems associated with using these tools to contract or expand the economy.

When the economy is in a recession, the Fed may engage in discretionary expansionary monetary policy. Usually the goal is to increase aggregate demand by increasing consumer or business spending (investment), which should move the economy toward full employment equilibrium. Historically, the Federal Reserve's actions to reduce or control inflation have often been more effective than its actions to stimulate the economy. Reducing the money supply and the subsequent increase in interest rates is usually very effective at reducing economic activity. Segment 3 also illustrates the effect of monetary policy on business decisions. You should be able to utilize the information in the video to draw an AS/AD graph explaining how monetary policy could affect the economy. This segment also presents some of the problems associated with discretionary monetary policy. What measures should the Fed target: Federal funds rate, M1, or M2? Time lags associated with monetary policy, as well as not having control over consumer or business behavior, are additional problems that limit the ability of the Fed to keep the economy at full employment.

As seen in the video, an especially difficult time for many people was the *stagflation* period in the 1970s and early 1980s. Stagflation represents an economy that is in a recession and therefore experiencing high rates of unemployment; however, the economy was also experiencing high rates of inflation. This time period was an exception to the fixed Phillips curve's inverse relationship between inflation and unemployment. Monetary policy that changed aggregate demand would have been inappropriate in this instance. Typically, if AD increases, then unemployment decreases, but price levels rise. If monetary policy decreases AD, then price levels fall, but unemployment rises. Therefore, any monetary policy that affects AD improves one problem (inflation or unemployment) while making the other one worse.

Segment 4 illustrates the equation of exchange $MV = PY$ (M = money supply, V = velocity, P = price level, Y = real GDP) and explains the concept of velocity and how velocity is determined. Some economists use Q to represent real GDP; therefore, the equation of exchange is sometimes represented as $MV = PQ$. There is disagreement over whether velocity is stable or variable. This question is important because the answer affects the ability of monetary policy to influence the macroeconomy.

LESSON ASSIGNMENTS

Text: Tregarthen and Rittenberg: *Macroeconomics*, Chapter 9, "The Nature and Creation of Money," pp. 197–200, and Chapter 11, "Monetary Policy and the Fed," pp. 223–244.

Video: "Monetary Policy" from the series *Choices & Change: Macroeconomics*.

LESSON OBJECTIVES

1. Define monetary policy.

2. Describe the goals of monetary policy.

3. List and define the policy tools of the Fed.

4. Explain the advantages and disadvantages of using each policy tool to alter the money supply.

5. Draw a graph to illustrate how the policy tools of the Fed are supposed to affect economic activity.

6. Explain monetary policy lags.

7. Explain how policy lags may impact the effectiveness of monetary policy.

8. Explain the rational expectations model.

9. Explain the potential effect of the rational expectations model on the effectiveness of monetary policy.

10. Draw a graph to illustrate how monetary policy can be offset by changes in investment.

11. Explain factors that determine velocity of money.

12. Use the equation of exchange with constant velocity to predict the effect of money supply changes on nominal income.

LESSON FOCUS POINTS

The following questions are designed to help you get the most benefit from the resources selected for this lesson. To maximize your learning experience:

  a. Scan the focus point questions.
  b. Read the assigned text pages.
  c. View the video.
  d. Write answers to the following questions. (References in parentheses can be used to locate information in the text and video that will help you answer the question.)

1. What is monetary policy and who is responsible for conducting it? (textbook, p. 161 and pp. 223–224; video segment 1)

2. What are the primary goals of monetary policy? Why are they important? (textbook, pp. 224–225; video segment 2)

3. Explain what tools of monetary policy the Fed can use to increase the money supply. Why would the Fed take these actions? (textbook, pp. 197–199; video segment 2)

4. If the Fed chose to decrease the money supply, explain what actions the Fed would take. What are the advantages and disadvantages of each tool of monetary policy? (textbook, pp. 197–199 and pp. 224–232; video segment 2)

5. Draw an aggregate supply and an aggregate demand curve. Also draw a graph of the money market. Show graphically what will happen if the Fed pursues expansionary monetary policies. Draw another set of curves and show graphically what will happen if the Fed pursues contractionary policies. (textbook, p. 228; video segment 2)

6. What factors can stall or delay the expected actions from monetary policies? (textbook, pp. 229–232; video segment 3)

7. Timing may be a problem in using monetary policy as a stabilization tool. The lags that may hinder the effectiveness of monetary policy as a stabilization tool are recognition, implementation, and impact lag. Explain the causes of these lags and briefly state how they could impair the effectiveness of monetary policy. (textbook, pp. 229–230; video segment 3)

8. What is the basic premise of the rational expectations hypothesis? (textbook, pp. 234–236; video segment 3)

9. Provide an example of how rational expectations may render monetary policies useless or ineffective in achieving their purpose. (textbook, pp. 234–236; video segment 3)

10. Construct a graph of investment demand and an AS/AD graph. Show graphically and briefly explain how changes in investment can offset the effects of expansionary monetary policy. (textbook, p. 234; video segment 3)

11. The following equation is referred to as the equation of exchange $MV=PY$. Define each of the variables in this equation and identify the factors that affect velocity and how they affect velocity. (textbook, pp. 236–238; video segment 4)

12. Assuming velocity is constant, illustrate mathematically how a change in the money supply would affect nominal GDP and income. (textbook, p. 238; video segment 4)

REVIEW

The following process is intended to help you retain the knowledge you have acquired in this lesson.

   a.   Review the terms and concepts highlighted in the textbook.
   b.   Review the checklists at the end of each section in the textbook.
   c.   Review the Case in Point examples in the textbook.
   d.   Review A Look Back in the textbook.
   e.   Complete the following Practice Test and check your responses.
   f.   Revisit the text and/or video for any questions you answer incorrectly on the Practice Test.

PRACTICE TEST

Multiple Choice: Circle the letter that corresponds to the BEST answer for each question.

1.   A primary goal of monetary policy is to
   A.   maintain high interest rates.
   B.   eliminate trade barriers from other nations.
   C.   prevent high rates of inflation.
   D.   reduce the size of the banking sector.
   E.   limit the availability of consumer credit.

2.   The tool of monetary policy that involves the Fed's buying and selling of government securities is
   A.   moral suasion.
   B.   reserve requirements.
   C.   the discount rate.
   D.   margin requirements.
   E.   open-market operations.

3.   In principle, if the Fed wants to reduce the money supply by discouraging depository institutions from borrowing reserves from Federal Reserve Banks, it could use
   A.   moral suasion.
   B.   reserve requirements.
   C.   the discount rate.
   D.   margin requirements.
   E.   open-market operations.

4. Which of the following tools is easily reversed if the Fed overshoots its target?
   A. Open-market operations
   B. Discount rate
   C. Reserve ratio
   D. All of the above
   E. None of the above

5. Which of the following tools would be difficult to reverse if the Fed overshoots its target?
   A. Open-market operations
   B. Discount rate
   C. Reserve ratio
   D. All of the above
   E. None of the above

6. The delay between the time at which an event occurs and the time at which policymakers become aware of it is the
   A. impact lag.
   B. political lag.
   C. implementation lag.
   D. government lag.
   E. recognition lag.

7. The shortest of the three lags for *monetary* policy is the
   A. political lag.
   B. implementation lag.
   C. recognition lag.
   D. government lag.
   E. impact lag.

8. The use of all available information to forecast future levels of economic activity and adjust behavior accordingly is
   A. monetary policy.
   B. fiscal policy.
   C. recognition policy.
   D. rational expectations.
   E. liquidity.

9. Which of the following would have the greatest impact on the effectiveness of monetary policy?
   A. Recognition lag
   B. Political lag
   C. Implementation lag
   D. Government lag
   E. Impact lag

10. When consumers and businesses utilize all available information and adjust their behavior accordingly, the result affects the ability of monetary policy to stabilize the economy. This refers to
    A. monetarism.
    B. the rational expectations theory.
    C. classical theory.
    D. all of the above.
    E. none of the above.

11. In the equation of exchange, the variable whose value must be computed from the other variables is the
    A. price level.
    B. quantity of output.
    C. quantity of money.
    D. velocity of money.
    E. interest rate.

12. If $V = 5$, $M = \$200$, and $P = \$2$, then Y is _____.
    A. 10
    B. 40
    C. 400
    D. 500
    E. 1,000

13. Which of the following does NOT affect velocity?
    A. Interest rates
    B. Bond prices
    C. Expectations
    D. Aggregate supply
    E. All of the above

14. If the velocity of money is constant, then a change in
    A. the money supply can be caused only by a change in real GDP.
    B. nominal GDP can be caused only by a change in the price level.
    C. M2 would always result in a larger percentage change in nominal GDP.
    D. M2 would always result in an equal percentage change in nominal GDP.
    E. the money supply can be caused only by a change in the price level.

Short-answer essay questions.

15. What is monetary policy, and who is responsible for implementing monetary policy?

16. Graphically illustrate and explain how expansionary monetary policy should affect the macroeconomy.

17. Continue with the example in question 16. Illustrate the effect of pessimistic business expectations on the effects of the expansionary monetary policy.

ANSWER KEY

1. C ....LO 2 .... Tregarthen/Rittenberg, pp. 223–225; video segment 2
2. E ....LO 3 .... Tregarthen/Rittenberg, pp. 198–199 and p. 225; video segment 2
3. C ....LO 3 .... Tregarthen/Rittenberg, p. 197
4. A ....LO 4 .... Tregarthen/Rittenberg, pp. 197–199
5. C ....LO 4 .... Tregarthen/Rittenberg, pp. 197–199
6. E ....LO 6 .... Tregarthen/Rittenberg, pp. 229–230; video segment 3
7. B ....LO 6 .... Tregarthen/Rittenberg, p. 230
8. D ....LO 8 .... Tregarthen/Rittenberg, p. 234; video segment 3
9. E ....LO 7 .... Tregarthen/Rittenberg, pp. 230–231
10. B ....LO 9 .... Tregarthen/Rittenberg, p. 234; video segment 3
11. D ....LO 11 .... Tregarthen/Rittenberg, pp. 237–238; video segment 4
12. D ....LO 11 .... Tregarthen/Rittenberg, pp. 237–238; video segment 4
13. D ....LO 11 .... Tregarthen/Rittenberg, pp. 236–238; video segment 4
14. D ....LO 12 .... Tregarthen/Rittenberg, p. 238; video segment 4

Short-answer essay questions.

15. LO 1 .... Tregarthen/Rittenberg, pp. 223–224; video segment 1
    Monetary policy is money and credit controls carried out by the Federal Reserve in order to encourage economic growth while maintaining price stability and low levels of unemployment.

16. LO 5 .... Tregarthen/Rittenberg, p. 227; video segment 2
    The Fed can choose open-market operations and buy bonds. This will increase the demand for bonds, causing an increase in bond prices. Increasing bond prices causes interest to decrease (Graph 1). Buying bonds also increases the money supply shown in Graph 2, which also decreases interest rates. Decreasing interest rates and increasing money supply cause spending or aggregate demand to increase. Graph 3 illustrates the movement toward full-employment equilibrium.

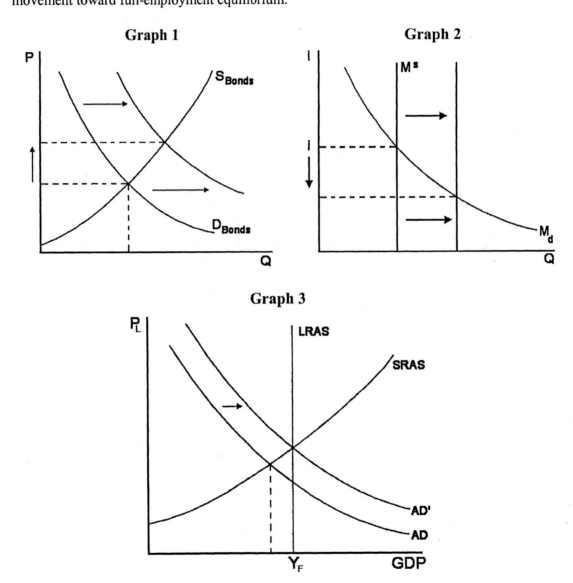

17. LO 10.................... Tregarthen/Rittenberg, pp. 234–236
Pessimistic business expectations will shift the investment demand curve to the left (decrease), which means even with lower interest rates, investment spending will not increase. Therefore, the aggregate demand curve will not shift toward full employment and may even decrease.

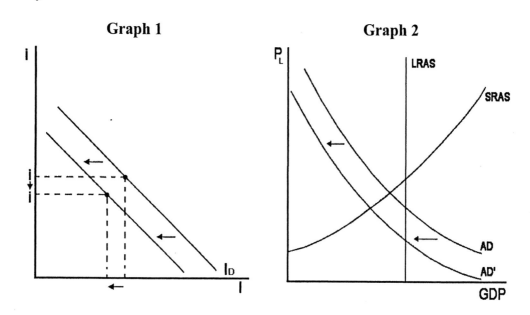

Graph 1   **Graph 2**

LESSON INTERVIEWEES

Michael F. Bryan, Assistant Vice-President and Economist, Applied Microeconomics Research, Federal Reserve Bank of Cleveland, Cleveland, OH

John B. Carlson, Economic Advisor, Research Department, Federal Reserve Bank of Cleveland, Cleveland, OH

Howard Hamilton, Executive Vice-President, McIlroy Bank & Trust Company, Fayetteville, AR

James A. Kornegay Jr., Tourist, Allen, TX

Wendy Lopez, President and CEO, Wendy Lopez & Associates, Inc., Dallas, TX

Robert D. McTeer Jr., President and CEO, Federal Reserve Bank of Dallas, Dallas, TX

Stephen Moore, Economist, The CATO Institute, Washington, DC

Libby Rittenberg, Professor of Economics, Colorado College, Colorado Springs, CO

Ed Stevens, Senior Consultant and Economist, Federal Reserve Bank of Cleveland, Cleveland, OH

Derek Thamm, Owner/Marketing Manager, Lubbock Feeders, L.L.C., Lubbock, TX

Lesson 11

Aggregate Expenditures

OVERVIEW

In previous lessons you have learned that $C + I + G + (X_n) = GDP$. Now we're going to look at the relationship between GDP spending (aggregate expenditures) and income at a fixed price level.

Recall that consumption is the largest component of aggregate expenditures (AE). Chapter 13 begins the AE model by developing the consumption function. The consumption function is an equation that relates consumer spending to the level of disposable income. Part of consumer spending, autonomous consumption (C_a), does not depend on income; however, most consumer spending does depend on income. Throughout this lesson the letter Y or Y_d denotes disposable income. The main part of the aggregate expenditures equation is the consumption function: $C = MPC(Y_d) + C_a$. MPC is the marginal propensity to consume and represents the percentage of an additional dollar of income that a consumer tends to spend. The remaining percentage is the marginal propensity to save (MPS). MPC + MPS always equals 1.

The next component of the AE model is planned investment (I_p). This is the part of aggregate expenditures that often has the greatest impact on the economy because it is the most volatile. Planned investment is the most volatile component since business expectations and subsequent reactions have a tremendous effect on the level of production, employment, and income in the economy. In this simplified model, planned investment does not depend on national income; therefore, it is autonomous. It is important to note that planned investment and actual investment may not be the same. Actual investment includes any unplanned changes in inventories. When adding investment to the AE model, the equation becomes $AE = MPC(Y_d) + C_a + I_p$. Any change in autonomous spending, C_a or I_p, has a multiplied effect on the macroeconomy. The simple spending multiplier = 1/MPS. By multiplying the change in autonomous spending by 1/MPS, the multiplied effect on equilibrium output and income can be calculated. Equilibrium output and income occurs when spending (AE) exactly equals the output produced in the economy.

Chapter 14 focuses on the investment component of aggregate expenditures and the factors that change planned investment. The video uses the roofing industry and the different businesses that contribute to a completed roof on your home to illustrate different types of investment. The video example also illustrates the multiplied effect of investment decisions on equilibrium output and income.

The last segment in the video adds net exports and government to the aggregate expenditures model. $AE = MPC(Y_d) + C_a + I_p + G + X_n$. These two components also have a multiplied effect on equilibrium income and output; however, changes in government taxing have a smaller multiplied effect than changes in government spending.

Note: In this lesson we concentrate on the AE model algebraically. The appendix to this lesson deals with the AE model graphically.

LESSON ASSIGNMENTS

Text: Tregarthen and Rittenberg: *Macroeconomics*, Chapter 13, "Consumption and the Aggregate Expenditures Model," pp. 267–289; Appendix 13, "Extensions of the Aggregate Expenditures Model," pp. 290–295; Chapter 14, "Investment and Economic Activity," pp. 296–309; and Chapter 15, "Net Exports and International Finance," pp. 310–329.

Video: "Aggregate Expenditures" from the series *Choices & Change: Macroeconomics.*

LESSON OBJECTIVES

1. Describe factors that determine the amount of consumption expenditure in the economy.

2. Determine the MPC, autonomous consumption, and induced consumption from a table or equation of the consumption function.

3. Explain why shifts in consumption occur.

4. Distinguish among investment, gross private domestic investment, net private domestic investment, and depreciation.

5. Explain the rationale for the inverse relationship between investment and the interest rate.

6. Interpret an investment demand curve.

7. Identify the factors that influence the level of investment.

8. Calculate the simple spending multiplier.

9. Explain the multiplier effect.

10. Use the multiplier to solve simple problems based on changes in autonomous expenditure.

11. Define equilibrium in the aggregate expenditures model.

12. Calculate equilibrium in an aggregate expenditures model.

13. Explain the impact of a change in investment on aggregate demand and on aggregate supply.

14. List the factors that affect net exports.

15. Explain the effects of government spending and taxing on the AE model.

16. Explain the effects of international trade on the AE model.

LESSON FOCUS POINTS

The following questions are designed to help you get the most benefit from the resources selected for this lesson. To maximize your learning experience:

a. Scan the focus point questions.
b. Read the assigned text pages.
c. View the video.
d. Write answers to the following questions. (References in parentheses can be used to locate information in the text and video that will help you answer the question.)

1. In terms of the consumption function, what determines consumer spending in the economy? (textbook, pp. 267–272; video segment 2)

2. If $C = .75(Y_d) + 200$, what is the marginal propensity to consume? What is autonomous consumption? What would induced consumption be if Y_d is 5,000? What is the sum of induced consumption and autonomous consumption? (textbook, p. 268 and pp. 274–276; video segment 2)

3. What factors cause consumption to change or shift? What factors would most likely change spending behavior? (textbook, pp. 270–272; video segment 2)

4. Define investment. What is depreciation and how does it relate to investment? (textbook, pp. 297–298; video segment 3)

5. All other things held constant (*ceteris paribus*), how would businesses react to falling interest rates in the economy? (textbook, pp. 301–302; video segments 3 and 4)

6. Recreate the graph of investment demand from the video lesson and explain what causes a movement along the curve and a shift in the curve. (textbook, pp. 276–277; video segment 3)

7. According to the interviewees in the video lesson, what are the most important factors that influence the level of investment? (video segment 3)

8. Calculate the spending multiplier in the economy if consumers spend three-fourths of additional income. What happens to the multiplier if the MPC increases? (textbook, pp. 278–279; video segment 4)

9. Given the spending multiplier from the previous question and a 200 billion (200^b) increase in autonomous expenditures, create a table similar to the one on page 278 in the Tregarthen/Rittenberg textbook. Calculate the process through six rounds. (textbook, p. 278; video segment 4)

10. Calculate the potential effect on GDP and income from the 200^b increase in autonomous expenditures by using the multiplier formula. Use the information from question #8. (textbook, pp. 278–279; video segment 4)

11. What is necessary for an economy to be in equilibrium? (textbook, pp. 276–277)

12. In the video, $AE = .8Y_d + 300^b + 400^b$

$$Y_d = .8Y_d + 700^b$$
$$.2Y_d = 700^b$$
$$Y_d = 3,500^b$$

equilibrium occurs when output, income, and spending are $3,500^b$ in the closed private economy. Calculate equilibrium if MPC increased to 90 percent. (textbook, pp. 274–275; video segment 4)

13. Due to optimistic business expectations there is an increase in investment. Graphically illustrate and explain how this would affect the aggregate demand and aggregate supply curve. (textbook, p. 278; video segment 4)

14. Net exports (X_n) are a component of aggregate expenditures. What factors change imports and exports? Explain how these factors affect X_n. (textbook, pp. 281–282; video segment 5)

15. Assuming that $AE = .75(Y_d) + 400^b + 100^b$ and government spending (G) is 200^b, calculate equilibrium income in the closed economy. What is the effect on equilibrium of adding 150^b in taxes (T)? (textbook, pp. 281–282; video segment 5)

16. Add X_n to the AE equation from the previous question. Explain what happens to equilibrium. (textbook, pp. 281–282; video segment 5)

REVIEW

The following process is intended to help you retain the knowledge you have acquired in this lesson.

a. Review the terms and concepts highlighted in the textbook.
b. Review the checklists at the end of each section in the textbook.
c. Review the Case in Point examples in the textbook.
d. Review A Look Back in the textbook.
e. Complete the following Practice Test and check your responses.
f. Revisit the text and/or video for any questions you answer incorrectly on the Practice Test.

PRACTICE TEST

Multiple Choice: Circle the letter that corresponds to the BEST answer for each question.

1. Household spending on goods and services is
   A. taxes.
   B. saving.
   C. exports.
   D. investment.
   E. consumption.

Income and Consumption

Disposable Income	Consumption
$ 100	$ 140
200	220
300	300
400	380
500	460

Use the table above to answer the following three questions.

2. When disposable income is $100, the MPC is approximately _____.
   A. 0.00
   B. 0.20
   C. 0.80
   D. 1.00
   E. 1.40

3. What is autonomous consumption?
   A. 0
   B. 20
   C. 60
   D. 300
   E. None of the above

4. What is consumption when Y_d = $1,000?
   A. $860
   B. $920
   C. $1,000
   D. $1,400
   E. None of the above

5. Given the consumption equation C = $500 + 0.8$Y_d$, if Y_d = $1,000, then induced consumption is _____.
   A. $300
   B. $500
   C. $800
   D. $1,000
   E. $1,300

6. Gross private domestic investment, the official government measure of investment, includes all of the following EXCEPT
   A. education.
   B. business structures.
   C. equipment.
   D. residential investment.
   E. changes in business inventories.

7. Investment is _____ spending on goods and services.
   A. foreign
   B. business
   C. household
   D. aggregate
   E. government

8. If gross private domestic investment exceeds depreciation, then
   A. net private domestic investment is positive.
   B. net private domestic investment is negative.
   C. the capital stock is declining.
   D. the capital stock is unchanged.
   E. education spending is rising.

9. A firm undertakes investment when
   A. the stock market looks favorable.
   B. it can buy plant and equipment cheaply.
   C. its rate of return on capital exceeds the rate of interest or cost of funds.
   D. the MPC exceeds its rate of return on capital.
   E. the interest rate is higher than the rate of return on capital.

Investment Projects

Project	Rate of Return	Cost
F	20%	$ 500
G	18	300
H	16	1,000
I	14	200
J	12	2,000
K	10	1,500
L	8	1,200
M	6	800

Use the table above to answer the following question.

10. If the market interest rate is 14 percent, planned investment expenditure is _____.
    A. $200
    B. $800
    C. $1,000
    D. $2,000
    E. $4,000

11. A decrease in investment demand can be caused by
    A. a decrease in the market interest rate.
    B. a decrease in corporate income tax rates.
    C. a decrease in the cost of new capital goods.
    D. a decrease in the expected demand of output.
    E. an increase in the rate of new technological innovations.

12. Other things remaining the same, a general decrease in the cost of new capital goods will typically
    A. have no effect on the level of investment.
    B. decrease total investment.
    C. shift the investment demand curve to the left.
    D. have no effect on the investment demand curve.
    E. increase the investment demand curve.

13. If the economy spends 80 percent of any increase in GDP, then an increase in investment of $1 billion results ultimately in an increase in GDP of _____.
    A. $0
    B. $0.8 billion
    C. $1.0 billion
    D. $1.8 billion
    E. $5 billion

14. The notion that a change in aggregate expenditures produces a larger change in equilibrium GDP in the aggregate expenditures model is called the
    A. permanent income effect.
    B. current income effect.
    C. multiplier effect.
    D. marginal expenditure rate.
    E. marginal propensity to consume.

15. In the aggregate expenditures model, equilibrium occurs if
    A. consumption equals investment.
    B. inventory changes equal saving.
    C. inventory changes equal investment.
    D. aggregate expenditures equal consumption.
    E. aggregate expenditures equal GDP.

16. If income increases in other countries, then U.S.
    A. imports increase.
    B. exports increase.
    C. imports decrease.
    D. exports decrease.
    E. imports and exports do not change.

17. If the U.S. exchange rate increases relative to currencies in other countries, then U.S.
    A. imports and exports both increase.
    B. imports and exports both decrease.
    C. imports decrease and exports increase.
    D. imports increase and exports decrease.
    E. imports and exports do not change.

Short-answer essay questions.

18. List the factors that change or shift consumption.

19. Utilize the investment demand curve below to determine investment if market interest rates are 6 percent.

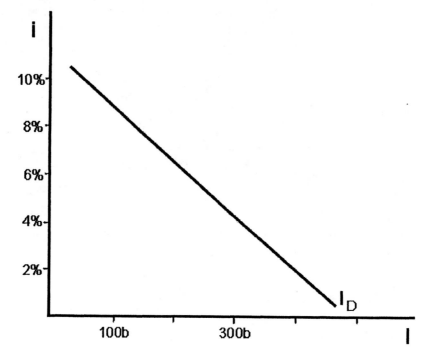

20. If $C = 0.6 Y_d + 300^b$, $I = 100^b$, $G = 50^b$ in a closed economy, calculate equilibrium income.

21. How does an increase in investment affect aggregate demand and aggregate supply?

22. Using the information in question #20, calculate the effect on equilibrium income from an increase in G of 100^b. Now in addition to the increase in G, calculate the change in equilibrium of an increase in T of 50^b.

ANSWER KEY

1. E ....LO 1 .... Tregarthen/Rittenberg, p. 267; video segment 1
2. C ....LO 2 .... Tregarthen/Rittenberg, p. 268; video segment 2
3. C ....LO 2 .... Tregarthen/Rittenberg, p. 268 and pp. 274–276; video segment 2
4. A ....LO 2 .... Tregarthen/Rittenberg, p. 268 and pp. 274–276; video segment 2
5. C ....LO 2 .... Tregarthen/Rittenberg, pp. 274–275; video segment 2
6. A ....LO 4 .... Tregarthen/Rittenberg, p. 297; video segment 3
7. B ....LO 1 .... Tregarthen/Rittenberg, p. 297; video segment 3
8. A ....LO 4 .... Tregarthen/Rittenberg, pp. 297–298
9. C ....LO 5 .... Tregarthen/Rittenberg, pp. 301–302
10. D ....LO 5 .... Tregarthen/Rittenberg, pp. 301–302
11. D ....LO 7 .... Tregarthen/Rittenberg, p. 302; video segment 3
12. E ....LO 7 .... Tregarthen/Rittenberg, p. 303; video segment 3
13. E ....LO 8, 10 .... Tregarthen/Rittenberg, pp. 278–279; video segment 4
14. C ....LO 9 .... Tregarthen/Rittenberg, p. 279; video segment 4
15. E ....LO 11 .... Tregarthen/Rittenberg, pp. 276–277
16. B ....LO 14, 16 .. Tregarthen/Rittenberg, pp. 312–313; video segment 5
17. D ....LO 14, 16 .. Tregarthen/Rittenberg, p. 313; video segment 5

Short-answer essay questions.

18. LO 3 .... Tregarthen/Rittenberg, pp. 270–272; video segment 2
    Consumption is the relationship between consumer spending and disposable income. Expectations and changes in real wealth will shift consumption.

19. LO 6 .... Tregarthen/Rittenberg, p. 301

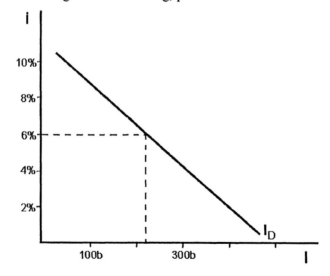

When interest rates are 6 percent, investment will be approximately 220^{b}, *ceteris paribus*.

---

20. LO 12 .... Tregarthen/Rittenberg, pp. 274–275; video segment 4

$Y = 0.6\,Y_d + 300^b + 100^b + 50^b$

$0.4Y = 450^b$

$Y = 1{,}125^b$

21. LO 13 .... Tregarthen/Rittenberg, p. 278 and pp. 306–307; video segments 3 and 4

The increase in investment will shift AD to the right by a multiple of the investment spending. If the increase in investment is 100^b and the spending multiplier is 4, then AD shifts right 400^b. The effect on AS will depend on the type of investment. If the investment is a technological improvement or increases production capabilities, then SRAS and LRAS will increase or shift to the right.

22. LO 15 .... Tregarthen/Rittenberg, pp. 274–275 and pp. 281–282; video segments 4 and 5

Previous equilibrium $Y = 1{,}125^b$

The spending multiplier equals 1/.4 which equals 2.5 and if G increases 100^b, then equilibrium increases by 250^b (100^b x 2.5). The new equilibrium is $1{,}125^b + 250^b = 1{,}375^b$.

If T increases 50^b, the tax multiplier is -1.5 and therefore, equilibrium decreases from 75^b to $1{,}300^b$.

LESSON INTERVIEWEES

Monty Banner, President, Ark Roofing, Inc., Irving, TX
Rhonda L. Brooks, President, Roofing Systems Business, Owens Corning, Toledo, OH
Sam F. Ciccarello, General Manager, Vigo Importing Company, Tampa, FL
Robert M. Dunn Jr., Professor of Economics, George Washington University, Washington, DC
Gus Herring, Economist, Brookhaven College, Farmers Branch, TX
Tom Motley, Professor of Art, Richland College, Dallas, TX
Louis-Paul Ricard, Sector Manager, Cargill, Inc., Tampa, FL
Chuck Sheffield, Professor of Art, Richland College, Dallas, TX
Holly St. Clair, Student, Tufts University, Medford, MA
John Yonkin, Southwest Regional Director, ABC Supply Company, Inc., Dallas, TX

Lesson 11—Appendix

Aggregate Expenditures

OVERVIEW

The aggregate expenditures model can be analyzed graphically. While there is some math involved, graphically finding equilibrium income and determining the changes to equilibrium from a spending change is often quicker than calculating it mathematically.

The graph's horizontal axis represents income and output while the vertical axis represents spending. The 45-degree (45°) line that bisects the axis represents income and spending and output combinations that are exactly in balance. This 45° line is, therefore, very useful in determining equilibrium.

The aggregate expenditures line is upward sloping with the slope being the marginal propensity to consume (MPC). The intersection of the aggregate expenditures line with the vertical axis represents autonomous spending. When the consumption (C) line intersects the 45° line, then C and Y_d are equal, which represents break-even income; for example, it represents the level of income where savings (S) equals zero. The point where the $C + I_p$ line intersects the 45° line represents an income and spending combination where savings (S) and investment (I_p) are equal. The point where the $C + I_p + G$ line intersects with the 45° line represents equilibrium in a closed economy, that is, no foreign trade. When AE includes consumption (C), investment (I_p), government (G), and net exports (X_n), and the AE line intersects the 45° line, that point represents an equilibrium among income, spending, and output in an open economy.

LESSON ASSIGNMENTS

Text: Tregarthen and Rittenberg: *Macroeconomics*, Chapter 13, "Consumption and the Aggregate Expenditures Model," pp. 267–289; Appendix 13, "Extensions of the Aggregate Expenditures Model," pp. 290–295; Chapter 14, "Investment and Economic Activity," pp. 296–309; and Chapter 15, "Net Exports and International Finance," pp. 310–329.

Video: "Aggregate Expenditures" from the series *Choices & Change: Macroeconomics*.

LESSON OBJECTIVES

1. Calculate investment, net exports, and government spending using an AE graph.

2. Label equilibrium on an aggregate expenditure curve.

LESSON FOCUS POINTS

The following questions are designed to help you get the most benefit from the resources selected for this lesson. To maximize your learning experience:

a. Scan the focus point questions.
b. Read the assigned text pages.
c. View the video.
d. Write answers to the following questions. (References in parentheses can be used to locate information in the text and video that will help you answer the question.)

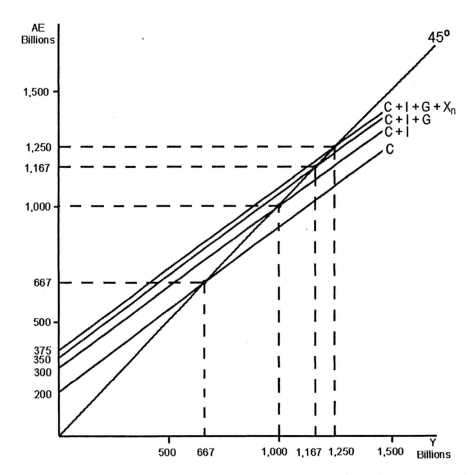

1. Use the graph above to determine the following amounts: (textbook, pp. 274–276; video segment 3)
   A. Autonomous consumption
   B. Autonomous investment
   C. Autonomous government
   D. Autonomous net exports
   E. Equilibrium income

---

2. Draw an AE curve to illustrate the example in the video. Graphically determine and label equilibrium in the "closed, private" economy. Graphically determine and label equilibrium in the "closed" economy. Graphically determine and label equilibrium in the "open" economy. (textbook, pp. 276–282; video segments 2 and 3)

REVIEW

The following process is intended to help you retain the knowledge you have acquired in this lesson.

    a.   Review the terms and concepts highlighted in the textbook.
    b.   Review the checklists at the end of each section in the textbook.
    c.   Review the Case in Point examples in the textbook.
    d.   Review A Look Back in the textbook.
    e.   Complete the following Practice Test and check your responses.
    f.   Revisit the text and/or video for any questions you answer incorrectly on the Practice Test.

PRACTICE TEST

Multiple Choice: Circle the letter that corresponds to the BEST answer for each question.

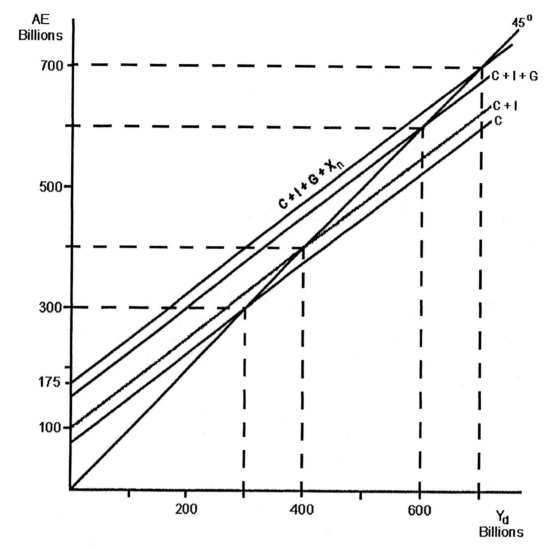

Use the graph above to answer all of the following questions.

1. Autonomous consumption is _____ billion.
   A. 0
   B. 50
   C. 75
   D. 100
   E. 300

2. Break-even income is _____ billion.
   A. 75
   B. 100
   C. 300
   D. 600
   E. none of the above

3. Autonomous investment is _____ billion.
   A. 25
   B. 100
   C. 400
   D. 600
   E. none of the above

4. Autonomous government spending is _____ billion.
   A. 25
   B. 50
   C. 100
   D. 150
   E. 600

5. Net export spending is _____ billion.
   A. 25
   B. 50
   C. 150
   D. 175
   E. 700

6. Savings is equal to investment when income is _____ billion.
   A. 50
   B. 300
   C. 400
   D. 600
   E. 700

7. Equilibrium in the "closed" economy is _____ billion.
   A. 300
   B. 400
   C. 600
   D. 700
   E. none of the above

8. Equilibrium in the "open" economy is _____ billion.
   A. 300
   B. 400
   C. 600
   D. 700
   E. none of the above

Short-answer essay questions.

9. Draw the graph that represents aggregate expenditures when $C = 0.6(Y_d) + 100^b$, $I_p = 75^b$, and $G = 25^b$.

10. Illustrate on the graph drawn for question #9 an increase in government spending of 50 billion. Graphically point out the change in equilibrium income from the increase in G.

ANSWER KEY

1. C ......LO 1 .... Tregarthen/Rittenberg, p. 274; video segment 2
2. C ......LO 2 .... Wyatt, telecourse guide Lesson 11—Appendix Overview
3. A ......LO 1 .... Tregarthen/Rittenberg, p. 274; video segments 1 and 3
4. B ......LO 1 .... Tregarthen/Rittenberg, p. 281; video segments 1 and 5
5. A ......LO 1 .... Tregarthen/Rittenberg, pp. 281–282; video segments 1 and 5
6. C ......LO 2 .... Wyatt, telecourse guide Lesson 11—Appendix Overview
7. C ......LO 2 .... Wyatt, telecourse guide Lesson 11—Appendix Overview
8. D ......LO 2 .... Wyatt, telecourse guide Lesson 11—Appendix Overview

Short-answer essay questions.

9.   LO 1.................... Tregarthen/Rittenberg, pp. 281–282; video segment 5

10.   LO 2.................... Tregarthen/Rittenberg, pp. 281–282; video segment 5

LESSON INTERVIEWEES

Monty Banner, President, Ark Roofing, Inc., Irving, TX
Rhonda L. Brooks, President, Roofing Systems Business, Owens Corning, Toledo, OH
Sam F. Ciccarello, General Manager, Vigo Importing Company, Tampa, FL
Robert M. Dunn Jr., Professor of Economics, George Washington University, Washington, DC
Gus Herring, Economist, Brookhaven College, Farmers Branch, TX
Tom Motley, Professor of Art, Richland College, Dallas, TX
Louis-Paul Ricard, Sector Manager, Cargill, Inc., Tampa, FL
Chuck Sheffield, Professor of Art, Richland College, Dallas, TX
Holly St. Clair, Student, Tufts University, Medford, MA
John Yonkin, Southwest Regional Director, ABC Supply Company, Inc., Dallas, TX

Lesson 12

Fiscal Policy

OVERVIEW

This lesson begins with a historical look at the U.S. national debt and then focuses on the effects of this debt on the macroeconomy. The national debt has often been a topic of debate, especially during election years. When this book was published, the U.S. national debt stood at nearly 5,700,000,000,000 dollars or $5.7 trillion, which is approximately $21,000 per man, woman, and child in this country. There is disagreement concerning how important the size of the debt is, as well as disagreement over who actually bears the burden of paying the debt. Is this level of debt a major concern for our economy? Opinions are quite varied on this subject. Make a note of your opinion on the subject prior to reading the rest of the material and viewing the video.

The third segment focuses on the fiscal policies during the Ronald Reagan administration and the development and use of supply-side economic theory. Some of Reagan's proposals were based on Arthur Laffer's work. The Laffer curve represents the relationship between marginal tax rates and tax revenue received by the government. If the government sets the marginal tax rate to the right of the curve's peak, then a decrease in tax rates leads to an increase in tax revenue. The major tax cuts during the Reagan administration were aimed at increasing the incentives to work, save, and invest. If taxpayers were to receive more of the income they earned, this in turn was supposed to cause tax revenues to rise. Again, there is disagreement over the validity of such an argument. Included in this segment is the compounding effects on the national debt of major tax cuts and increased military spending during the 1980s.

The last segment presents the fiscal policies and promises of the Bush and Clinton administrations in the 1990s and the effects on economic growth and the national debt. One of the most important concepts in this lesson is that the state of the economy, good or bad, is often a result of the actions or inaction of a past president, his administration, and particularly of Congress. Praising or blaming a current administration for the state of the economy is often undeserved.

LESSON ASSIGNMENTS

Text: Tregarthen and Rittenberg: *Macroeconomics*, Chapter 12, "Government and Fiscal Policy," pp. 245–265.

Video: "Fiscal Policy" from the series *Choices & Change: Macroeconomics*.

LESSON OBJECTIVES

1. Distinguish between the following pairs: government purchases and government spending, and expansionary and contractionary fiscal policies.

2. Explain the difference between the deficit and the debt.

3. Explain how changes in the following affect aggregate expenditures: personal income taxes, transfer payments, business taxes, payroll taxes, and government purchases.

4. Utilize AS/AD curves to illustrate fiscal policy effects.

LESSON FOCUS POINTS

The following questions are designed to help you get the most benefit from the resources selected for this lesson. To maximize your learning experience:

    a. Scan the focus point questions.
    b. Read the assigned text pages.
    c. View the video.
    d. Write answers to the following questions. (References in parentheses can be used to locate information in the text and video that will help you answer the question.)

1. List two examples of government purchases and two examples of government spending that are not purchases. How do these differ? (textbook, p. 127 and pp. 246–247)

2. List two examples of expansionary fiscal policy and two examples of contractionary fiscal policy. Describe how these examples will work to expand or contract the economy. (textbook, p. 250 and pp. 252–255)

3. Use the AS/AD model to illustrate the effects of the expansionary and contractionary fiscal policy examples from question #2. Highlight the effects on equilibrium price levels and equilibrium output levels. (textbook, pp. 252–255)

4. Explain why some federal deficits are unavoidable. Compare a deficit created when an economy is in a recession to a deficit created when an economy is expanding. What is the importance of the difference? (textbook, pp. 256–257)

5. How does the federal government create the national debt? (textbook, p. 249 and pp. 258–259; video segment 2)

6. Aggregate expenditures are equal to $C+I_g+G+X_n$. What happens to AE when there are increases in each of the following: personal income taxes, transfer payments, business taxes, payroll taxes, and government purchases. (textbook, pp. 252–255)

REVIEW

The following process is intended to help you retain the knowledge you have acquired in this lesson.

a.   Review the terms and concepts highlighted in the textbook.
b.   Review the checklists at the end of each section in the textbook.
c.   Review the Case in Point examples in the textbook.
d.   Review A Look Back in the textbook.
e.   Complete the following Practice Test and check your responses.
f.   Revisit the text and/or video for any questions you answer incorrectly on the Practice Test.

PRACTICE TEST

Multiple Choice: Circle the letter that corresponds to the BEST answer for each question.

1.   Public investment expenditure for highways, schools, and national defense is included in _____ purchases.
   A.   household
   B.   investment
   C.   government
   D.   consumption
   E.   net export

2.   Expansionary fiscal policy includes
   A.   decreasing taxes.
   B.   increasing taxes.
   C.   decreasing the money supply.
   D.   increasing the money supply.
   E.   decreasing government expenditures.

3.   Contractionary fiscal policy includes
   A.   decreasing taxes.
   B.   decreasing the money supply.
   C.   increasing the money supply.
   D.   decreasing government expenditures.
   E.   increasing government expenditures.

4. If the government's total revenue is greater than total expenditures, then it has a budget
   A. deficit.
   B. surplus.
   C. balance.
   D. equality.
   E. equilibrium.

5. A deficit
   A. exists when government revenues exceed government spending.
   B. is the sum of all past government spending less any repayments.
   C. only occurs when an economy is in a recession.
   D. exists when government spending exceeds government revenue.
   E. none of the above.

6. Transfer payments
   A. typically rise during expansionary periods.
   B. typically fall during recessions.
   C. do not change as the economy expands and contracts during the business cycle.
   D. fall during expansionary periods and rise during contractionary periods.
   E. have no impact, one way or another, on the level of expenditures.

7. If the federal government increases purchases, then a likely result is
   A. an increase in real GDP.
   B. a decrease in consumption.
   C. an increase in unemployment.
   D. a decrease in the price level.
   E. a decrease in aggregate demand.

8. If the federal government increases business taxes, then a likely result is
   A. an increase in real GDP.
   B. a decrease in investment.
   C. an increase in unemployment.
   D. a decrease in the price level.
   E. a decrease in aggregate demand.

9. If the federal government decreases income taxes, then a likely result is
   A. an increase in real GDP.
   B. a decrease in consumption.
   C. an increase in unemployment.
   D. a decrease in the price level.
   E. a decrease in aggregate demand.

10. An increase in payroll taxes will
    A. shift the SRAS curve to the right.
    B. increase employment.
    C. decrease cost per unit of labor.
    D. decrease real GDP.
    E. decrease the price level.

Short-answer essay questions.

11. Compare your pre-lesson opinion on the national debt with your after-lesson opinion.

12. Explain the difference in the deficit and the debt in terms of personal finance.

13. Draw an AS/AD graph to illustrate the effect from question #7.

14. Draw an AS/AD graph to illustrate the effect from question #8.

15. Draw an AS/AD graph to illustrate the effect from question #9.

16. Based on the video "Fiscal Policy," graphically illustrate the effects on the macroeconomy from actions taken during the Reagan administration.

17. Based on the video "Fiscal Policy," graphically illustrate the effects on the macroeconomy from the actions taken to reduce the deficit during the Bush administration.

ANSWER KEY

1. C ....LO 1 .... Tregarthen/Rittenberg, p. 127 and pp. 246–248
2. A ....LO 1 .... Tregarthen/Rittenberg, p. 250 and pp. 253–254
3. D ....LO 1 .... Tregarthen/Rittenberg, p. 250 and pp. 253–254
4. B ....LO 2 .... Tregarthen/Rittenberg, p. 248; video segment 2
5. D ....LO 2 .... Tregarthen/Rittenberg, p. 248; video segment 2
6. D ....LO 3 .... Tregarthen/Rittenberg, p. 247
7. A ....LO 3 .... Tregarthen/Rittenberg, p. 246 and p. 252
8. B ....LO 3 .... Tregarthen/Rittenberg, p. 253; video segment 3
9. A ....LO 3 .... Tregarthen/Rittenberg, pp. 253–254; video segment 3
10. D ....LO 3 .... Tregarthen/Rittenberg, p. 248 and pp. 252–255

Short-answer essay questions.

11. LO 2 .... Tregarthen/Rittenberg, pp. 245–265; video segment 2
Answers will vary.

12. LO 2 .... Tregarthen/Rittenberg, pp. 248–249; video segment 2
When you spend more dollars than your income in a given time period, then you incur a deficit. The borrowing to pay for the spending that exceeds income added to past borrowing less any reductions or payments on the debt represents total debt. Borrowing includes credit card balances which are part of consumer debt.

13. LO 4 .... Tregarthen/Rittenberg, pp. 252–253

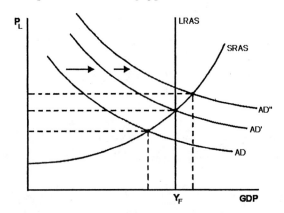

An increase in government purchases will shift AD to the right. If the economy was experiencing a recessionary gap, then the increase to AD' would close the recessionary gap. If the economy was at full employment and AD' shifted to AD", then an inflationary gap would be created.

14. LO 4 .... Tregarthen/Rittenberg, pp. 252–253; video segment 3

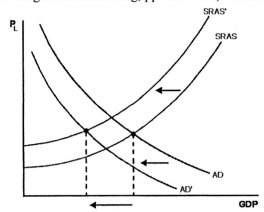

An increase in business taxes will probably decrease AS since cost of production would rise. An increase in business taxes would also decrease AD since investment would decrease. The overall effect on the price level would depend on the extent to which these curves shift. Both changes would likely either cause a recession or intensify a recession.

15. LO 4 .... Tregarthen/Rittenberg, pp. 252–253; video segment 3

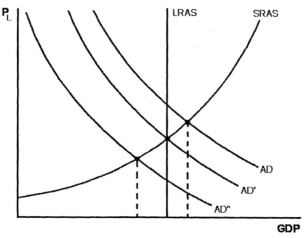

An increase in income taxes would cause a decrease in AD since consumers would have less income to spend. If the economy was experiencing an inflationary gap, then the decrease in AD would bring the economy back toward full-employment equilibrium. If the economy was at full employment or experiencing a recessionary gap, then the decrease in AD would either cause a recession or deepen the existing recession.

16. LO 4 .... Tregarthen/Rittenberg, pp. 252–253 and p. 257; video segment 3

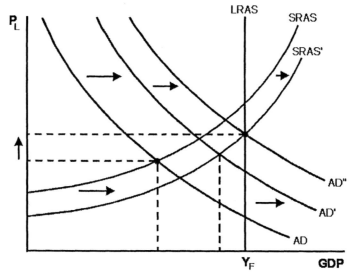

The tax cuts were supposed to increase both aggregate supply and aggregate demand. There were also some major increases in government spending on the military. This also increased aggregate demand.

17. LO 4 .... Tregarthen/Rittenberg, p. 250 and p. 252; video segment 4
President Bush's tax increases caused a decrease in aggregate demand and higher rates of
unemployment.

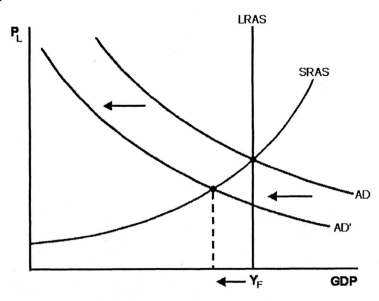

LESSON INTERVIEWEES

Frank Ackerman, Research Assistant Professor, Department of Urban and Environmental
      Policy, Tufts University, Medford, MA
Diana Furchgott-Roth, Resident Fellow, American Enterprise Institute, Washington, DC
Philip Seib, Political Analyst, WFAA-TV, Dallas, TX
Timothy Tregarthen, Economist/Author, University of Colorado, Colorado Springs, CO

Lesson 13

Schools of Thought

OVERVIEW

The evolution of economic thought is as dynamic as the macroeconomy that it tries to explain. This lesson deals with the major macroeconomic theories that have influenced government decisions for the past 100 years. Remember from Lesson 4 that economies go through phases of the business cycle, alternating between periods of expansion and contraction.

Prior to the Great Depression, classical economic theory was generally accepted in the United States as explaining how an economy works. In this theory, if an economy is experiencing either an inflationary or a recessionary period, then flexible wages, prices, and interest rates will adjust to bring the economy back to full-employment equilibrium. Classical economics adequately explained the behavior of the economy until the Great Depression, when some things seemed to change. Classical economists argued that actions taken by the government and Federal Reserve intensified the Depression and that if the government had not disrupted the adjustment process, then the Depression would not have been so severe. The second segment looks further at the disagreement over the causes as well as the "cure" for the Great Depression.

The third segment continues with a historical view of macroeconomic theory from post–World War II through the Reagan administration in the 1980s. During this period, the Phillips curve was developed to represent the inverse relationship between unemployment and inflation. The Phillips curve theory held until the United States experienced a period of *stagflation*, which is simultaneous high unemployment and high inflation. This period led to *supply-side* economic theory, which is often referred to as "Reaganomics." "Trickle-down," which is another way of expressing a multiplier effect, was an expression sometimes used to refer to Reaganomics. In other words, government actions to stimulate economic activity and, at the same time, lower inflation rates, were meant to flow through the economy down to the lower income levels. This was to be accomplished by cutting marginal tax rates to stimulate working, saving, and investment and, therefore, to create jobs. Recall from Lesson 12 that the idea of cutting marginal tax rates came from Arthur Laffer, who argued that tax rates were too high. In his opinion, if the government cut tax rates, the effect would be to increase the incentive to work more since less of the income would go to the government. Laffer also argued that decreased tax rates and increased work would cause government tax revenues to rise. This segment also looks at how successful supply-side theory was in the 1980s.

The focus of the last segment is economic theory in the last decade of the twentieth century. For the most part, the economy grew and expanded while keeping inflation very low, once again violating the logic of the fixed Phillips curve. The Federal Reserve's policies have been both credited and criticized during this period.

LESSON ASSIGNMENTS

Text: Tregarthen and Rittenberg: *Macroeconomics*, Chapter 16, "Inflation and Unemployment," pp. 330–349, and Chapter 17, "A Brief History of Macroeconomic Thought and Policy in the 20th Century," pp. 350–371.

Video: "Schools of Thought" from the series *Choices & Change*: *Macroeconomics*.

LESSON OBJECTIVES

1. Explain why unemployment and inflation may rise or fall together at times, while at other times they move in opposite directions.

2. Describe the phases of the inflation-unemployment cycle.

3. Explain why the long-run cause of inflation is generally agreed to be excessive monetary growth.

4. Discuss disagreements over the monetary policy actions of the Fed.

5. Identify the economic growth effects of different monetary and fiscal policies.

6. Evaluate the likely impact on growth from a proposed set of policy actions.

7. Explain the relationship between saving and economic growth.

8. Describe the differences and similarities in the basic beliefs of monetarists and new classicals.

9. Predict policy positions of the different schools of economic thought in dealing with economic problems.

LESSON FOCUS POINTS

The following questions are designed to help you get the most benefit from the resources selected for this lesson. To maximize your learning experience:

a. Scan the focus point questions.
b. Read the assigned text pages.
c. View the video.
d. Write answers to the following questions. (References in parentheses can be used to locate information in the text and video that will help you answer the question.)

1. The Phillips curve model suggests there is a tradeoff between inflation and unemployment. What are the reasons for this tradeoff? (textbook, p. 331; video segment 3)

2. Stagflation is simultaneous high inflation and high unemployment. What are the causes of stagflation? What is the cure for stagflation? (textbook, pp. 338–339; video segment 3)

3. The three phases of the inflation-unemployment cycle are the following: the Phillips phase, the stagflation phase, and the recovery phase. Briefly explain what is happening to inflation and unemployment for the three phases of the inflation-unemployment cycle. Be sure to explain why inflation and unemployment rates are changing. (textbook, pp. 333–338; video segment 3)

4. How does excessive monetary growth affect the macroeconomy? (textbook, p. 340; video segment 4)

5. The Fed has been regarded as the guardian against inflation. The Fed is also an independent government agency whose primary purpose is to promote economic stability. In the video "Schools of Thought," what are the common criticisms leveled against the Fed? (video segment 4)

6. What are expansionary monetary and fiscal policies? When are they used and what do they entail? What will happen to output levels when they are used? What will happen to the level of spending in the economy when they are used? (textbook, pp. 355–356; video segment 2)

7. What are contractionary monetary and fiscal policies? When are they used and what do they entail? What will happen to the level of spending in the economy when they are used? (textbook, pp. 357–358; video segment 4)

8. Economic growth can be defined as increases in real GDP over time. Briefly explain some economic policies that facilitate or promote economic growth. (textbook, pp. 362–367; video segment 4)

9. Savings is a prerequisite for investment and provides funds that can be made available for producing capital goods. How do savings and investments affect economic growth? (textbook, pp. 355–367; video segments 3 and 4)

10. What are the basic beliefs of the monetarist school of economics? How does monetarism compare to the basic beliefs of the new classical school of economics? (textbook, pp. 359–360; video segment 4)

11. Briefly outline the different policy positions for the various macroeconomic theories or schools of thought in regard to reducing inflation and unemployment rates. (textbook, pp. 355–367; video segments 3, 4, and 5)

REVIEW

The following process is intended to help you retain the knowledge you have acquired in this lesson.

    a.   Review the terms and concepts highlighted in the textbook.

    b.   Review the checklists at the end of each section in the textbook.

    c.   Review the Case in Point examples in the textbook.

    d.   Review A Look Back in the textbook.

    e.   Complete the following Practice Test and check your responses.

    f.   Revisit the text and/or video for any questions you answer incorrectly on the Practice Test.

PRACTICE TEST

Multiple Choice: Circle the letter that corresponds to the BEST answer for each question.

1.   Suppose the economy experiences an increase in the unemployment rate at the same time the inflation rate declines. This situation indicates a

    A.   shift in the short-run Phillips curve.

    B.   movement along the vertical long-run Phillips curve.

    C.   movement along the horizontal long-run Phillips curve.

    D.   movement along the positively sloped short-run Phillips curve.

    E.   movement along the negatively sloped short-run Phillips curve.

2.   Other things remaining the same, an economy is better off on

    A.   the highest possible Phillips curve.

    B.   the top left of a given Phillips curve.

    C.   the bottom right of a given Phillips curve.

    D.   a lower Phillips curve than a higher Phillips curve.

    E.   a higher Phillips curve than a lower Phillips curve.

3.   In the 1970s, the U.S. economy

    A.   shifted to a lower Phillips curve.

    B.   shifted to a higher Phillips curve.

    C.   moved along a short-run Phillips curve.

    D.   moved along a long-run Phillips curve.

    E.   exhibited no tradeoff between unemployment and inflation.

4.   The short-run Phillips curve would shift up due to

    A.   a decrease in the actual rate of inflation.

    B.   an increase in the actual rate of inflation.

    C.   a decrease in the expected rate of inflation.

    D.   an increase in the expected rate of inflation.

    E.   a decrease in the natural rate of unemployment.

5. The pattern of a Phillips phase, stagflation phase, and recovery phase observed in the relationship between inflation and unemployment is termed the
   A. inflation-unemployment cycle.
   B. stagflation-efficiency cycle.
   C. Phillips curve cycle.
   D. business cycle.
   E. circular flow cycle.

6. The Phillips phase of the inflation-unemployment cycle emerges because
   A. prices and wages are flexible.
   B. nominal wages and prices fall.
   C. resource prices are lower.
   D. people recognize the overstimulation of the economy and reduce spending.
   E. people are surprised by price increases produced by increases in aggregate demand.

7. The stagflation phase of the inflation-unemployment cycle is explained by shifts to the
   A. right in the SRAS curve.
   B. left in the SRAS curve.
   C. right in the LRAS curve.
   D. left in the AD curve.
   E. right in the AD curve.

8. Evidence suggests that all countries with higher _____ also have higher _____.
   A. money growth rates; unemployment rates
   B. unemployment rates; GDP growth rates
   C. GDP growth rates; government budget deficits
   D. government budget deficits; inflation rates
   E. inflation rates; money growth rates

9. The long-run aggregate supply curve would shift left if
   A. consumption expenditures declined.
   B. aggregate demand increased.
   C. higher taxes discouraged investment.
   D. the supply curve for labor increased.
   E. prices for natural resources decreased.

10. Fiscal and monetary policy can be used to promote economic growth by
    A. decreasing interest rates.
    B. discouraging savings.
    C. reducing spending on infrastructure.
    D. expanding the federal budget surplus.
    E. increasing unemployment.

11. Fiscal and monetary policy can be used to promote economic growth by
    A. increasing interest rates.
    B. discouraging savings.
    C. increasing spending on infrastructure.
    D. expanding the federal budget surplus.
    E. increasing unemployment.

12. In general, an economy that saves more today will
    A. show an increase in consumption today.
    B. show a decrease in consumption in the future.
    C. be able to produce less real output in the future.
    D. be able to produce more real output in the future.
    E. cause the production possibilities curve to shift inward.

13. New classical economics is based on the proposition that
    A. prices and wages are sticky.
    B. output seldom achieves full employment.
    C. business cycles are good for the economy.
    D. people make logically reasoned forecasts from existing information.
    E. changes in the money supply have a direct impact on changes in the price level.

14. New classical economics contends that policy activism is
    A. not warranted because we do not know enough about the workings of the economy to stabilize it.
    B. not warranted because the public defeats discretionary policies since everyone expects them, and therefore, their effectiveness is thwarted.
    C. not warranted since discretionary policies have no effect on real output.
    D. warranted because expectations are rational only in the short run.
    E. warranted because expectations are rational only in the long run.

15. The ability of the economy to adjust its natural level of employment on its own
    A. would bring about an increasing role in government fiscal policy.
    B. would bring about an increasing role in the Federal Reserve's monetary policy.
    C. would have a major impact on U.S. international trade policy.
    D. is the heart of a fundamental disagreement among economists about the role of public policy.
    E. is an issue addressed by economists.

Short-answer essay question.

16. From the video "Schools of Thought," characterize the different opinions concerning active monetary policy carried out by the Federal Reserve.

ANSWER KEY

1. E ....LO 1 .... Tregarthen/Rittenberg, p. 331; video segment 3
2. D ....LO 1 .... Tregarthen/Rittenberg, p. 331; video segment 3
3. B ....LO 1 .... Tregarthen/Rittenberg, pp. 332–334; video segment 3
4. D ....LO 1 .... Tregarthen/Rittenberg, pp. 335–337; video segment 3
5. A ....LO 2 .... Tregarthen/Rittenberg, p. 333
6. E ....LO 1, 2 ...... Tregarthen/Rittenberg, p. 337
7. B ....LO 1, 2 ...... Tregarthen/Rittenberg, p. 337; video segment 3
8. E ....LO 3 .... Tregarthen/Rittenberg, pp. 340–341
9. C ....LO 5 .... Tregarthen/Rittenberg, p. 355; video segment 3
10. A ....LO 6 .... Tregarthen/Rittenberg, pp. 355–356; video segments 2 and 3
11. C ....LO 6 .... Tregarthen/Rittenberg, pp. 353–356; video segments 2 and 3
12. D ....LO 7 .... Tregarthen/Rittenberg, pp. 353–356
13. D ....LO 8 .... Tregarthen/Rittenberg, p. 360
14. B ....LO 8 .... Tregarthen/Rittenberg, pp. 360–361
15. D ....LO 9 .... Tregarthen/Rittenberg, p. 367

Short-answer essay question.

16. LO 4 .... Tregarthen/Rittenberg, pp. 365–367; video segment 4

Some argue that the Fed's actions cause many of our macroeconomic problems. For example, during the Great Depression, many banks were allowed to fail and the money supply decreased. The Fed also increased the reserve ratio. These actions turned what could have been a long recession into the Great Depression.

Today, there is disagreement over whether the Fed should engage in active monetary policy. For the most part, there seems to be agreement that inflation is primarily a monetary phenomenon. Whether monetary policy can strongly affect economic activity is still debated.

LESSON INTERVIEWEES

Jeff Carbiener, Adjunct Professor of Economics, Southern Methodist University, Dallas, TX

John B. Carlson, Economic Advisor, Research Department, Federal Reserve Bank of Cleveland, Cleveland, OH

Robert D. McTeer Jr., President and CEO, Federal Reserve Bank of Dallas, Dallas, TX

Ester-Mirjam Sent, Assistant Professor, University of Notre Dame, Notre Dame, IN

Lesson 14

Economies in Transition

OVERVIEW

Market capitalism and command socialism are extremes of the economic spectrum. All economic systems have elements of both capitalism and socialism; that is, there are varying degrees of socialism mixed into capitalist systems and vice versa. The most significant difference between capitalism and socialism is the ownership or control of productive resources. Economic systems usually evolve slowly over time, but sometimes there are violent upheavals. This lesson looks at examples of both changes.

Japan is one example of a market capitalist country with a significant level of government involvement in the economy. At the beginning of the twenty-first century, Japan was characterized by few natural resources, major import barriers, and cooperation between business and government. Japan has had a system where occupations and careers have often been predetermined by tradition. This segment also illustrates the brief history of the Soviet Union, which was created in the violent Russian Revolution of 1917. Following the revolution, the Soviet Union became the premier example of a command economy where the government decided how productive resources would be used and how output would be distributed. This was an extremely difficult task considering the Soviet Union was geographically over twice the size of the United States with enormous amounts of productive resources. This segment also explores the varying levels of government involvement in the economy in other countries, including the United States.

The third segment presents an interesting social experiment that was very successful in helping Israel increase its productive capacity and standard of living. The Kibbutzim, which began in the early 1900s, were instrumental in the survival of Israel. They turned a barren, rock-laden desert into a productive agrarian base. More recently, the Kibbutzim have expanded into manufacturing and tourism.

The evolution of the Cuban economy is the focus of the last segment. After centuries of Spanish rule, Cuba became independent with the aid of the United States. In the late 1950s, Cuba became a command-base economy with the takeover by Fidel Castro. The success of Castro's regime was due in large part to aid from the Soviet Union. When the Soviet Union dissolved, Cuba lost a major supporter. Now, Cuba must try to maintain its economy without massive aid.

All economic systems are combinations of market capitalism and command socialism. And macroeconomies continue to experiment, change, and evolve.

LESSON ASSIGNMENTS

Text: Tregarthen and Rittenberg: *Macroeconomics*, Chapter 19, "Economic Development," pp. 394–414, and Chapter 20, "Socialist Economies in Transition," pp. 415–431.

Video: "Economies in Transition" from the series *Choices & Change: Macroeconomics*.

LESSON OBJECTIVES

1. Define market (capitalist) and command types of economic systems.

2. Examine socialism in action.

3. Explore the history of utopian societies.

4. Explore some of the economic successes and failures of countries that have experienced major changes in their economic focus.

LESSON FOCUS POINTS

The following questions are designed to help you get the most benefit from the resources selected for this lesson. To maximize your learning experience:

   a. Scan the focus point questions.
   b. Read the assigned text pages.
   c. View the video.
   d. Write answers to the following questions. (References in parentheses can be used to locate information in the text and video that will help you answer the question.)

1. Use examples from the video "Economies in Transition" to explain how market capitalism differs from command socialism. (video segment 2)

2. Utilize information from the textbook and the video to present an argument for or against command socialism based on the successes and failures. (textbook, pp. 394–431; video segments 2, 3, and 4)

3. What are some of the problems associated with Cuba's loss of Soviet aid? What is the country doing to survive the loss? (video segment 4)

4. Compare the Kibbutz concept to Marxian ideas. (textbook, pp. 416–418; video segment 3)

5. Name some countries that have experienced major changes in economic focus. In other words, what countries have undergone fundamental changes in regard to owning property resources and how resources are allocated? Briefly comment on their experience with these changes. (textbook, pp. 419–429; video segments 2 and 4)

REVIEW

The following process is intended to help you retain the knowledge you have acquired in this lesson.

    a.   Review the terms and concepts highlighted in the textbook.
    b.   Review the checklists at the end of each section in the textbook.
    c.   Review the Case in Point examples in the textbook.
    d.   Review A Look Back in the textbook.
    e.   Complete the following Practice Test and check your responses.
    f.   Revisit the text and/or video for any questions you answer incorrectly on the Practice Test.

PRACTICE TEST

Multiple Choice: Circle the letter that corresponds to the BEST answer for each question.

1. An economic system in which most capital is privately owned and allocative decisions are made by the private sector is
    A.   market commandism.
    B.   command socialism.
    C.   market socialism.
    D.   command capitalism.
    E.   market capitalism.

2. Countries with the highest average standard of living follow
    A.   market commandism.
    B.   command socialism.
    C.   market socialism.
    D.   command capitalism.
    E.   market capitalism.

3. In the late twentieth century, Japan was characterized by
    A.   abundant mineral resources.
    B.   very little cooperation between business and government.
    C.   high barriers to imports.
    D.   a civil service system that is independent of business.
    E.   low per capita production.

4. In the late twentieth century, Japan was characterized by
   A. abundant mineral resources.
   B. extensive cooperation between business and government.
   C. almost no barriers to imports.
   D. a civil service system that is independent of business.
   E. low per capita production.

5. The economy of Sweden is characterized by
   A. limited income redistribution programs.
   B. historically low living standards.
   C. very little government involvement in the economy.
   D. high tax rates.
   E. indicative planning.

6. Centrally controlled economies had moderate success in achieving the goals of
   A. equity and growth.
   B. equity and stability.
   C. growth and stability.
   D. efficiency and growth.
   E. efficiency and stability.

7. An evaluation of centrally planned economies reveals that they have
   A. put a premium on technological innovation.
   B. achieved a nearly equal distribution of income.
   C. been successful in attaining economic efficiency.
   D. experienced production rigidities and shortages.
   E. experienced higher rates of inflation than most capitalist countries.

8. Central control proved to be a failure in communist countries because of
   A. abundant market information.
   B. unquestioned reliance on the price system.
   C. excessive incentives for economic growth.
   D. insufficient use of government ownership.
   E. inadequate rewards for innovation.

Short-answer essay questions.

9. Briefly describe the attempts at utopian societies presented in the video "Economies in Transition."

10. Explain where a Kibbutz falls in the economic spectrum between socialism and market capitalism.

ANSWER KEY

1. E ....LO 1......... Tregarthen/Rittenberg, p. 54 and p. 407; video segment 2
2. E ....LO 1......... Tregarthen/Rittenberg, pp. 407–411; video segment 2
3. C ....LO 2......... Wyatt, telecourse guide Lesson 14 Overview
4. B ....LO 2......... Wyatt, telecourse guide Lesson 14 Overview; video segment 2
5. D ....LO 2......... video segment 2
6. B ....LO 4......... video segments 2 and 4
7. D ....LO 4......... Tregarthen/Rittenberg, p. 420
8. E ....LO 4......... Tregarthen/Rittenberg, pp. 419–423

Short-answer essay questions.

9. LO 3 .... video segment 3
The concept of a utopian society has been around for thousands of years. The French revolution and later the Russian revolution were driven by the desire of many to have a more equitable system. "Hippie" communes in the United States were based on utopian ideas. The video highlights one of the most successful attempts at a utopian society, the Kibbutz.

10. LO 1, 4 .... Tregarthen/Rittenberg, pp. 416–417; video segment 3
The Kibbutz system is very unusual. It is based on the Marxian concept of contributing what you can and only taking what you need. What's left is used to expand the community. What's unusual is this very socialist ideal is governed in a very democratic manner. Everything is done for the good of the community, but it is the individuals in the community that make the decisions by democratic voting.

LESSON INTERVIEWEES

Steven L. Cobb, Chair, Department of Economics, University of North Texas, Denton, TX
Barry L. Duman, Ph.D., Professor of Economics, West Texas A&M University, Canyon, TX
Luis Locay, Associate Professor, University of Miami, Coral Gables, FL
Annette Morganstern, Director, American Zionist Movement, Dallas, TX
David L. Ramsour, President, Texas Council on Economic Education, Houston, TX
Jorge A. Sanguinetty, President, DevTech Systems, Inc., International Economic Consultant, Washington, DC